FIRST
INTELLIGENCE

PRAISE FOR *FIRST INTELLIGENCE*

"*First Intelligence* takes the intuitive skill set out of the clouds and brings it firmly down to earth. Simone Wright provides an objective framework and process, backed by grounded science, that explains that everyone has the ability to make powerful decisions and important actions using this innate level of wisdom. It is an important read for those brave enough to explore the power they possess."

— MIKE SAUNDERS, detective, Calgary Police Service

"*First Intelligence* is the owner's manual for the Ferrari you didn't even know you owned. You were born fully equipped to live an intuitively guided life; all you need is someone to point out your gear and show you how to use it. Simone Wright breaks intuition down in a straightforward way, removing labels like 'esoteric' or 'New Age' and placing it firmly in the realm of everyday experience. A fascinating, rewarding read!"

— ALISON LAVENTHOL, TV writer, *Fairly Legal* and *Perception*

"Combining the practical and the mystical, *First Intelligence* is a top-rate guide that brings the often misunderstood realm of intuition into a grounded yet dynamic understanding that we all can and should be excited to develop. It is an elegant combination of science and spirit." — EVELYN PUNCH, MSc, neuroscience

"Simone Wright has produced a handbook for a new way of living, with practical advice on how to reawaken the first intelligence we so often suppress. She uses language that is down-to-earth and accessible, and she references scientific studies as well as her time teaching members of the police force, which all adds to the grounded credibility of her advice. If you want to further your journey and access your intuition but don't want the fluff, then this book is for you."

— MANJIR SAMANTA-LAUGHTON, MD, author of *Punk Science* and *The Genius Groove*

FIRST
INTELLIGENCE

USING THE
SCIENCE & SPIRIT
OF INTUITION

SIMONE WRIGHT

New World Library
Novato, California

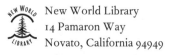 New World Library
14 Pamaron Way
Novato, California 94949

The material in this book is intended for education. No expressed or implied guarantee of the effects of the use of the recommendations can be given nor liability
taken. Some names have been changed to protect the privacy of individuals.

Text design by Tona Pearce Myers

Library of Congress Cataloging-in-Publication Data
Wright, Simone, date.
First intelligence : using the science and spirit of intuition / Simone Wright.
    pages   cm
Includes bibliographical references and index.
ISBN 978-1-60868-246-1 (pbk. : alk. paper) — ISBN 978-1-60868-247-8 (ebook)
1. Intuition. I. Title.
BF315.5.W75 2014
153.4'4—dc23   2014000365

First printing, June 2014
ISBN 978-1-60868-246-1
Printed in the USA on 100% postconsumer-waste recycled paper

 New World Library is proud to be a Gold Certified Environmentally
Responsible Publisher. Publisher certification awarded by Green Press
Initiative. www.greenpressinitiative.org

10 9 8 7 6 5 4 3 2 1

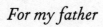

For my father

CONTENTS

PART IV. PLAYING IN THE INTUITIVE FIELD

PREFACE

Miracles are not contrary to nature, but only contrary to what we know about nature.

— SAINT AUGUSTINE

"Three and three." It was the second time in one day I had heard those words.

Those three words were the first impression I received as I stepped into the nondescript Vietnamese restaurant in a nondescript strip mall in a nondescript part of town. The walls of the restaurant were painted a sunny, butter yellow, and there was an aquarium filled with fish by the front door. In the Asian art of feng shui, the symbolic energies of the color yellow and the living fish are used to generate happiness, harmony, and prosperity, but they did little to disguise the flurry of unsettling images and feelings that inundated me as I stepped into the foyer.

I had been dropped off at the restaurant by a police detective friend of mine. Knowing of my skills as an intuitive, he had invited me on a field test to give my abilities a workout and see what, if anything, I could come up with.

Mark had been a police officer for over twenty years and had spent much of that time undercover and as a detective specializing in drugs, vice, and homicide. He had phoned earlier that day with an assignment for me. The call was unexpected because I was in town for only about twelve hours during a layover on my way back to Los Angeles after teaching a weekend intuition workshop in Canada.

Being careful not to divulge too much detail, Mark informed me he would be picking me up in a couple of hours to "take me to a scene." That was it. No further details; no other clues. No sooner had the statement left his mouth than the words *three and three* flashed in my mind, along with an overwhelming sense of unease. I knew instantly that what lay ahead was not going to be a walk in the park. And I knew with even more certainty that more than one person involved was dead.

My Beginnings

I have been highly intuitive and perceptually aware my entire life. The varied experiences of my childhood might be called paranormal or psychic, but these out-of-the-ordinary occurrences never struck me as odd. They were more inconvenient than anything else, because as a child I hadn't understood them. Only as I have gotten older have I been able to appreciate their value and to recognize the power of what I was capable of doing.

The first intuitive experience that I clearly remember happened when I was about seven years old. I had been using my abilities before that time to help me navigate life, but this one incident stands out in my mind as the beginning.

My father was dying. The testicular cancer had been diagnosed less than a year earlier, and while the initial tumors had been removed, his disease was aggressive and had begun a quick and destructive march through the rest of his body. At the early age of thirty-three, my handsome, athletic, and powerful father, who should have been living the best years of his life, was living the last days of it instead.

Both of my parents did their best to shelter my younger brother and me from the realities of our father's illness, but I knew the truth of the matter was that his days were numbered. My rare hospital visits were occasions filled with a mixture of anticipation and dread; I missed my dad and I wanted him to come home, but I also knew that something was terribly, terribly wrong and I didn't know what to do about it.

The last time I saw my father alive, I stood tentatively in the corner of the hospital room, unsure what to say or do. I was nervous and afraid to approach him, but it wasn't just because of the tubes and wires embedded in his body or because I knew he was in pain; the thing that kept my feet glued to the floor was the fact that I could see through him. When I would look at my father, he was transparent.

I could clearly see the dials and knobs of his monitoring equipment mounted on the wall directly behind him as he sat propped up against his pillow. Reflecting on that experience now, I know I was observing his life force leaving his body, rendering it, to my sensitive perceptions, "less there."

I didn't say anything to either of my parents about what I saw. In fact, in childhood I never spoke to any of the adults in my life about what I could see, sense, or feel, because I was afraid I would get in trouble for it. And in later years I often did get in trouble for it. This ability to see through people as they approach death continues to this day.

The following evening as I was drifting off to sleep, I was awakened by a bright blue glow at the foot of my bed. It was a vivid, sparkling aquamarine color, and it took form as though a bright fog had entered the room. I couldn't tell where it had come from or how long it had been there, but it hovered for a time as if waiting for me to completely wake and acknowledge it. I felt no fear. The glow, almost liquid in nature, began to speak, not in words, not in measurable sound, but in thought form, a telepathy of sorts. The message, the feelings, the images I saw in my mind's eye were those of my father. He had come to say farewell.

"Simone," he said, "I wanted to come and say good-bye. It's time for me to go. I want to let you know how much I love you, how much I care for you, and how very sorry I am that I have to leave you right now. But I want you to know that whenever you need me, I will be here watching over you, and if you ever need my help, all you need to do is call on me and I will be there. I love you, my sweetie. Be a good girl for your mom. I'll miss you. I'm sorry. Good-bye." The blue glow faded, and he was gone.

The next morning my mother returned from the hospital carrying a single red rose and called me into her bedroom. She sat me on the foot of the bed and handed me the rose saying, "Sweetie, I have to tell you that Daddy won't be coming home anymore. He has passed away. He has gone to heaven."

It sounded like she was a million miles away, and I recall feeling as though a part of me vanished in that moment, but I also was aware that I already knew what she was saying was true. "I know, Mommy, I know," I said. "He came to me last night and said good-bye."

I don't really remember much after that moment. The shock of losing a husband and father quickly set in, and we had many things to take care of and a new normal to cultivate. I never mentioned the visitation by my father to anyone again.

My heightened perceptions intensified as I grew older. Most people, especially adults, were particularly difficult for me to be around. I could feel their moods, and, for a kid, their anger and frustration were tough to tolerate. So I remained pretty isolated. I would spend hours a day holed up in my bedroom drawing, painting, and playing with my pets.

I was raised Catholic and went to Catholic school. The nuns

who were my instructors said I was difficult to teach, and I would get in trouble or be overlooked a lot because I was so quiet. All the while, I sensed things that none of the teachers could have understood.

I knew that the majority of what I was being taught in school and was required to believe in church simply wasn't the truth. When I did find the courage to open my mouth to challenge dogma or question the status quo, either in school or in my family, I was quickly and painfully reminded that such queries were a symptom of defiance and willfulness and would not be tolerated. The reminder, especially at school, often came in the form of an eighteen-inch rubber eraser wielded across my back by the unflinching Sister Caroline. It took a while but eventually I learned how to become invisible and keep my visions and "knowings" to myself.

In my midteens I began to intentionally reject my abilities and did everything I could to turn the volume down on them. By the time I hit my twenties I had pretty much forgotten them, and I did my best to live as normal a life as possible. It was emotionally and physically impossible to keep my abilities bottled up, though — sort of like trying to plug a volcano with a wine cork. But I didn't know what else to do about them. When I was in my midtwenties, my life began to spiral out of control when the denial that I had adopted for so long simply didn't work anymore. I couldn't pretend to be someone I wasn't, regardless of the consequences.

At the lowest point of my darkest days, my father kept the promise he made to me the night he appeared at the foot of my bed. He would prove to be the linchpin between me and what would soon become an important part of my destiny.

AN INTUITIVE REBOOT

In the winter of 1998 I decided to return home for a Christmas visit with my family. At the time, I was in a tailspin. I had no relationship with my intuition, and all memories of my youthful skills and experiences had been neatly and deeply buried away.

During a break in the holiday festivities with family, I took a couple of hours to visit my father's gravesite, which I hadn't done in almost twenty years. As I sat alone in my mother's car overlooking the cemetery, I spoke aloud all the words and emotions that I had bottled up for so long. I told my father how much I missed him and hoped that he was well wherever he was. Tears were pouring down my face, and snot was streaming over my chin, and all I could do was be with the words and emotions I was putting out into the world. In a moment of deep and heartfelt desire to connect with my father and find some peace with my feelings of loss, I asked aloud the question "Why weren't you there for me, Daddy?"

And then, there it was, as clear as a bell over my right shoulder, from the seat behind me. A voice. A low, quiet voice that said, "I have been here the whole time. You just weren't listening."

I spun around to look in the backseat, knowing full well I wouldn't see anyone there, but I felt more strongly than I ever had before that I wasn't alone. In that moment I felt as though the top of my head blew open and all the memories of my psychic childhood experiences came flooding back to me. In what I can describe only as an instant informational download, I remembered all the things I had worked so hard to forget.

For a second I tried to convince myself that I was making it all up, but I also recognized the familiar feeling of denial that had haunted me for so long, and I knew I could no longer continue the charade. I was too tired to fight it anymore; so there in the icy fields of Saint Mary's Cemetery, I surrendered to the energy that I had kept stuffed away for more than a decade and had a beautiful conversation with my long-dead father.

When the conversation ended and my dad's energy evaporated from the car, I sat numb for almost an hour trying to process and integrate everything that had just happened. I don't remember the drive home. When I finally returned to my mother, she asked, "How'd it go?"

The only thing I could manage to say to her was: "Good. It went good."

My questions for my father had been answered, and life for me would never be the same.

FIELDWORK

The owner of the restaurant was a tiny man with a kind face, and he greeted me at the host's desk, asking if I wanted a table. He didn't know who I was or why I was there; in fact, at that precise moment even I didn't know why I was there. And if I had known, how would I have explained it to him, anyway?

It would have been strange to come into his place of business and not get anything to eat, so I ordered some noodles and chicken to go. While I waited, I sat at a small table and casually scanned the room and then pretended to read a menu. My order took less than ten minutes to prepare, but that was more than enough time for me to get what I needed. I thanked the host. Based on what I felt, I knew he had been through a lot.

Mark was waiting for me outside. I climbed into the car and, holding my fingers up, said, "Three."

He nodded silently.

The information played itself out like a movie in my head in a rapid-fire succession of images. I let the perceptions flow — no editing, no thinking, no rationalizing, interpreting, or second-guessing. First impressions are the only impressions that I give voice to. I say it as I see it.

"Three inside. Three outside. Two hit inside. One hit outside. The one hit outside didn't belong. He was in the wrong place at the wrong time, an innocent bystander. This was a gang hit. The victims knew their assassins. Little guy in first. He held the door for the big guy, who came in second. Both shooting. Two different guns, nine-millimeter semiautomatic.

"Bang. Bang. Bangbangbang. Woman screams. Third guy outside. Parked in a silver car. Waiting at the far end of the parking lot. Southwest side. Snowy. Gray. Icy. He didn't know what was going to happen but went along with it anyway. Wasn't in on the plan."

I went on to give detailed physical descriptions of the shooters and a general description of the driver, as well as information about possible hiding spots for the weapons that were used. Gradually the information trickled to a stop. I felt energized by the process, but I felt sad for everyone involved.

Mark remained stoic as I rattled off the information, never once indicating whether I was hot or cold. He was good at not giving anything away.

It was obvious to me by now that this had been a triple homicide, a gang-related hit that turned the restaurant into its killing ground. There were three victims and three perpetrators. Now I understood what was meant by my earlier impression "three and three."

"Well," Mark said. "Pretty impressive. You were spot-on. I'd say you had 90 to 95 percent accuracy on what we already know. You even had the 'holdback.'"

The "holdback," I would learn, is the information that law enforcement knows about a case but never releases to the public or the media; they "hold it back." This information may be what they use to break a case or to secure a suspect — crucial secret details that only someone who had been at the scene of the crime would know. He continued: "Even though I know you didn't — because I didn't even tell you where we were going today — you could have used Google or something to get your intel. But holdback is big —

there's no way you could have gotten *that* from Google or anywhere else." He's such a cop.

We sat together in silence for a little while, and then Mark said, "Say, would you be interested? I mean, would you want to do this work for the police department full-time?"

I laughed and without hesitation said, "*Hell no!*"

In a case like this one, I sense and feel everything — the fear, the anger, the sadness, and the residual confusion. Sometimes I feel the pain of a victim and the shame of a perpetrator. I knew I simply wouldn't be able to handle it full-time. But before I knew what I was saying, I blurted out, "But what if I could teach the cops to do what I do? Intuition, I mean. Would that interest you?"

Mark looked at me like I had two heads. "You can do that? This stuff can be taught?"

"Yes."

"You don't have to be gifted or psychic or spiritual or special?"

"No. Anyone can do it. We are born to do it. I mean, maybe not exactly the way I do it, but everyone can develop their natural skills to use in life. That's what I teach in my workshops. This intelligence is in our biology. It's a head-heart thing. Not a voodoo, woo-woo thing. The teaching process might be different for cops, because they need more facts, but I can teach anyone to do it."

Within two months of my intuitive fieldwork with Mark, two arrests were made in the triple-homicide case. Within six months a third arrest had been made. All three suspects went to trial and are now serving life sentences. Nine months after that meeting with Mark, I was in a room with twenty-two seasoned police detectives from various departments teaching them how to do what I do. For the cops, that meant how to use their intuition to assist them in solving cases, to communicate more effectively with witnesses, to discover new theories about a crime, and to stay healthy and reduce stress.

But for many other people, that means accessing their highest wisdom to achieve greater financial security or to make the most potent decision about which career path is in their best interest. And for some, it may be about making powerful health choices or determining what is best for a relationship. The opportunities to put intuition to work are unique and as limitless as the individuals who use it, and these opportunities are shaped only by their desires and dreams. The power of intuition is our spiritual and material birthright, and learning how to use it is more important now than ever before.

INTRODUCTION

THE POWER OF FIRST INTELLIGENCE
CREATING A NEW PARADIGM

Cease trying to work everything out with your minds. It will get you nowhere.
Live by intuition and inspiration and let your whole life be a revelation.

— EILEEN CADDY

I ntuition is a survival tool. I invite you to let go of the warm, fuzzy, New Age, hippie idea of what you may have thought it was in the past, and to consider a broader, more grounded and practical approach to what it really is and how you might use it in your life. Intuition is not an ethereal, magical skill. It is an intelligence.

I have come to call this intelligence "First Intelligence" because it develops long before we possess the ability to reason or learn anything the external world has to teach us, and it is in operation before we even know that we *can* know. It is the intelligence of life. Intuition is specific and precisely tuned to each one of us as individuals, and it guides each of us to our highest potential.

Intuition does *not* rely on previous knowledge; it does not find its information in studies, research, analysis, graphs, or statistics. True intuition (which is *not* the same thing as instinct) seeks the routes, solutions, and innovations that align with the potential of our evolution and guides us beyond the tired, worn, unproductive patterns of our past.

Intuition works hand in hand with imagination, innovation, inspiration, and intent, gently leading us to see from a different perspective all the things that we experience. Whether this means a crisis in our health or a relationship, a fork in a career or life path, or an opportunity to create success and great abundance, our intuition is ready to guide us to the attitudes, actions, and alliances that will make the most of each of those situations. All the while, it ensures that we maintain our highest level of survival and most powerful evolutionary potential.

Held within every cell of our body and guided by an innate desire to thrive, intuition is a multifaceted and multidimensional guidance system. It uses not one particular sense, one particular part of the body, or one level of the mind to cultivate its outcomes but rather the entire structure of the human being — mind, body, and spirit — to provide direction and inspiration.

In order to fathom the power of our intuition, we must understand that it is a completely normal human function that works both within and outside our physical body. It uses all our energetic and biological equipment in the exact same way that every other biological function does, to support our survival and provide us with the best outcomes for life.

Many people connect with that inner voice of wisdom for the first time, only to run from it afterward, never to return, convinced that what they were doing was dangerous or abnormal. Others seek medical or psychiatric assistance, certain they are mentally ill, and are prescribed drugs to quiet that inner voice and lock the door of that intelligence. The initial surprise when First Intelligence reveals itself often blocks a person's desire to continue to engage in the intuitive relationship.

There is a solid middle ground between science and spirit,

between the visible and the invisible, and the finite and the infinite, and it holds answers to questions about both sides of the discussion. Intuition falls evenly and elegantly onto both sides and, as a result, proves that it can serve both the material and the spiritual aspects of who we are as human beings.

As I noted earlier, first intelligence is a normal human function. There are many attributes and levels of communication — chemical, emotional, physical, and energetic — and they are all happening at the same time. These functions of intelligence are not supernatural. They are natural. They are not paranormal. They are normal. We simply need to remember how to use them.

Evolving into the Intuition Age

We are exposed to more types of media and more information than any generation before us. According to a study done at the University of Southern California, the average person processes the equivalent of 174 newspapers' worth of data per day. Add to that the rise in email and social media, and the twenty-four-hour news cycle, and we are being inundated with over five times the amount of data people were receiving less than twenty years ago.[1] Today when we have a question about anything, from money and health to relationships, success, and family, we can, with the click of a button, find countless pages and innumerable voices full of information on it. But this overload of information can shift us into analysis paralysis and downgrade our intelligence by amplifying our worry and anxiety.

So how do we survive this tsunami of data to discover if any of it is based even slightly in real intelligence? How do we learn how much of it is true and how it applies to us, or whether any of it serves our best interests?

In order to survive the acceleration in external technology, we are going to have to accelerate the development of our *internal* technology. The good news is that it is already happening. We already possess the technology we need, and the power of life is already guiding us in how to use it. It's up to us to learn to listen to this guidance and follow the directions.

WE'VE ALL GOT IT

We all have the ability to use our intuition, but in order to be *actively* intuitive — which means to be able to use it at will instead of by happenstance — we must develop the skill. Think of developing your intuition as being like learning a new language: everyone has the capacity for it, but to achieve fluency you must study a language's rules, understand its principles, and practice it on a regular basis. You must be willing to go out into the world and use it and develop a feel for it, and you must also get comfortable with getting it wrong a few times. We learn just as much by recognizing what doesn't work as we do by recognizing what does.

Everybody has the ability to develop this powerful skill, but not everybody has the dedication and patience necessary to master its subtle nature. You won't get good at it by simply reading this book or by talking about it with your friends or by sitting around and meditating about it all day long. You will have to go out there and figure out what works for you and what doesn't. You will have to want to discover what feels right and what doesn't feel right. You will need to become intimate with what you felt, did, or noticed when you were successful, and what you did that caused you to land face-first in the mud. You need to be willing to get your intuitive hands dirty, because living intuitively is no place for sissies.

The rewards gleaned from consistent practice are incalculable, and the time you dedicate to consideration and application of the principles of First Intelligence will reward you in ways that you previously may not have considered.

LIFE ACCORDING TO WHOM?

Every single one of us has experienced intuition in our lives. Whether you are an entrepreneur, a stay-at-home parent, or a police detective, there have been moments when you had a subtle yet undeniable hunch or deep gut instinct that turned out to be correct — a knowing without knowing how you knew.

Some people let such moments of expanded perception pass by without much notice. For others, these moments make an indelible impression that drives them to understand and use them to improve their lives. When I ask people why they want to develop their intuition, they often say, "I want to know if this is the life that I am *supposed* to be living." Or: "I want to know if my spouse is the person I am *supposed* to be with, or if my job is the one I am *supposed* to have."

There seems to be a universal human need to know or believe that what we are doing in our lives is appropriate or good, a need to have some sort of seal of approval from a higher, external standard. Parents maybe. Society possibly. Karma perhaps.

But the question is: "supposed to have or be" according to whom? Certainly every opportunity we experience is a chance to gain greater wisdom, but choosing to believe that certain things happen to us because "God or Spirit" says so, that we have no choice in the matter, is an error of monumental proportion. Such a belief would leave us to assume that divine intelligence exists outside of us, and that we as beings who possess consciousness and free will are meant to blow like leaves on an unpredictable wind. But as mystics have taught for centuries, and as science is gradually validating, this simply is not the case.

Intuitive intelligence gives us the power to choose our destiny and create it as a matter of focused and directed will. This wisdom does not happen *to* you; it takes shape *in* you and *through* you. Through every organ, cell, and strand of DNA, it links you to the field of universal intelligence and can connect you to whatever you may desire for yourself.

What you desire for yourself is what it desires for you, so that you can be happy, continue to grow, and experience life in all the ways you have dreamed of. The only thing you *should* be doing is living your life in a way that supports you in greeting every day with joy, peace, and purpose. Life wants you to be healthy, abundant, successful, filled with love, and constantly expanding, because those are the very principles of life itself. And if your joy lies in being a sanitation worker or a surgeon, an artist or an accountant; or in being in a relationship or out of one; or in living in a mansion or a small studio, then that is what you *should* be doing.

You get to decide, because *you* are the only one here.

First Intelligence serves the power of our own unique choices, and it uses every aspect of our humanity to do so. But it requires us to first develop the courage to commit ourselves to making those choices.

LETTING GO OF WHAT WE KNOW

My mission in life is to reassure people from all walks of life that intuition is not a mind trick that some people have access to and some people do not. It is a natural and obvious tool that keeps us constantly and continuously linked to the answers we seek and the perfect guidance we need in any situation.

Intuition is specific, designed exclusively for each individual. My intuition guides *me* based on what I need to reach my highest potential. Your intuition guides *you* based on what you need to reach your highest potential. It cannot and does not serve more than one master. This is why those who are committed to following the guidance of their intuitive voice often leave others confused, baffled, irritated, or convinced that they have truly lost their minds! Those who are not connected to the power of their highest wisdom simply cannot grasp the realities that seem so obvious to those who *are* connected. And so they do their best to convince themselves that the geniuses and the dreamers, the artists and the visionaries, are fools at best and madmen at worst.

Becoming a creative genius in your own life does not require you to become more intelligent or to gather more knowledge. All it requires is that you allow your intuition and imagination to guide you, and that you believe absolutely nothing is impossible. Many of the most revolutionary visionaries throughout time who have gone on to change how we experience the world — including Michelangelo, Leonardo da Vinci, Richard Branson, Steve Jobs, Henry Ford, and Galileo — depended on something greater, grander, and more compelling than most of us are used to, but it made all the difference in their lives and ours. If they hadn't followed their hearts and listened to the subtle voice of their intuitive First Intelligence, what would our world look like? If you were brave enough to follow yours, what would your life look like?

It does not matter if anyone else understands your vision for the future. The connection you have with your own inner sight is the only thing that has power. If, in your mind's eye, you can see your vision for your life, and you can feel it in your heart, then regardless of what anyone else may see or understand, it can and will become a reality.

Intuition is *not* a product of the human brain or intellect. Your brain, what you know, what you have been taught, your IQ, your GPA — none of these will help you with your intuition. They simply aren't powerful enough. Our intuition will say, "Leap. Jump. Go for it. Let go of what is known. You will be safe." But then our intellect talks us out of it by saying, "What will people think? How will I pay my bills? It will never work. I can't." So we don't, and life stays the same.

How many times have you allowed fear or faithlessness to hit the mute button on your highest intelligence? You aren't alone, because we have all done it. The truth of the matter is, if you want to be a visionary in your own life — that is, to see potentials and possibilities for the future that do not exist now — you must be willing to take some chances and let go of what feels safe and known. If you want your life to evolve, you'd better jump. You may never be certain about where you will end up, but your heart, your courage, and your intuition will always guarantee that what you see from your new perspective will not be the same as before. The human heart is the hub of intuitive intelligence, and creativity, innovation, passion, and vision radiate out from it like the spokes of a magnificent wheel constantly rolling toward higher ideals and greater potential.

Relying on your intuition is simple, but rarely is it easy. Intuition requires courage in every moment, because it leads you to take risks, to act entirely on faith. It supplies no proof, no outward sign that you are about to do the right thing. And while the details of how you develop and refine your intuitive power should be addressed at first with a fair bit of consideration, I invite you to engage in the process with a light touch. Maintain a sense of ease and play — this is a natural skill, after all, so you need not approach it as if it were a precious thing.

WHAT TO EXPECT FROM THIS BOOK

Consider making *First Intelligence: Using the Science and Spirit of Intuition* your user's manual for your intuition. I have tried to include only relevant information that will teach, inspire, elevate, and amaze you as you learn about the intuitive process and how to use it as a guide to any outcome you desire. You do not have to be anything or anyone other than who you are in this moment in order to have it work for you. To be successful in this, you need only the desire to amplify the wisest part of yourself and to take action in the ways that I suggest in these pages.

Everything I have included here, with the exception of the stories provided by some of my students as examples, I have had direct experience with, both personally and professionally. Nothing is presented as a philosophy, theory, or conjecture. It is important to me to share with you only information that is practical and applicable to your own life. And the only way I could be certain of doing that was by testing it, teaching it, experimenting with it, and evaluating it in the laboratory of life.

The information, insight, and practice included here proceed in a way that assumes you and I are in agreement about intuition, and that, to some degree, you already accept it as a reality. Your goal is to have a deeper understanding of what intuition is and how it works, and to develop and refine your skill so you can use it in more specific and powerful ways to serve your life and improve your future. Let's get started.

PART I

THE BIOLOGY
OF INTUITION

Living in the Material World

CHAPTER 1

YOUR TRILATERAL INTELLIGENCE SYSTEM

Look deep into nature and then you will understand everything better.
— ALBERT EINSTEIN

Research has begun to prove that we are born with what I call "First Intelligence," an innate and powerful guidance system that ranges from the wisdom inherent in the tiniest strand of DNA to the advanced intelligence discovered in the chambers of the heart. First Intelligence is wired deeply in every cell we possess, and it uses our DNA to connect us *to* and communicate *with* the same intelligence that guides the planets and gives birth to all the stars in the universe.

THE HUMAN GPS

The fact is, your intuition is working for you already, in everyday situations, *without* your knowing a single scientific detail about how or why it works. But knowing how it works helps you use it more effectively and removes any superstition or stigma attached to what, up until now, may have been perceived as supernatural or otherworldly.

Our intuition is housed in every cell of our body and continually responds to the information and energies in our environment every moment of our lives. We literally have everything we need within our biology to be powerfully intuitive almost from the moment of conception.

The human body possesses what I call its Trilateral Intelligence System, which uses its trillions of cells to operate as a biological antenna, transmitter, and receiver. It is our own biological GPS and can easily be used to guide us to well-being, success, and lifelong happiness. Our First Intelligence operates in exactly the same way.

If you don't believe that the invisible transmission of information is a possibility, just think about how many times you have used a cell phone or wireless Internet connection. Human beings likewise have the ability to invisibly transmit and receive information, but we are also gifted with a powerful consciousness that can guide and manipulate our human technology in ways that no piece of machinery ever will.

The Trilateral Intelligence System of each person is based in the brain, the gut, and the heart, and it is uniquely equipped to perceive, gather, and share information that can and will guide us wherever we wish to go. It doesn't require us to be special or gifted or spiritually evolved; all it requires is that we be human.

I invite you to take a moment to make sure you have everything you need. Brain? Check! Gut? Check! Heart? Check! Okay, with that concern taken care of, there is absolutely no reason for you to doubt your ability to access your intuitive intelligence. The only thing for you to do now is to learn how to use it.

Our Biological Brilliance

As human beings we are born to be highly intelligent and highly creative intuitive intelligence machines. The statement that we human beings use less than 10 percent of our intelligence is generous at best. I believe it is more accurate to say we use less than 5 percent of our "brilliance potential." If we could get all our intelligence systems aligned and working toward our chosen highest good, the things we could do for ourselves and for the world would be mind-boggling.

In this chapter, we will focus on *form.* I will outline the biology of each system and show how it is structured to gather information from our environment. We will examine the *function* of all the moving parts in later chapters, when we discuss in detail how each system specifically translates that information into intuitive guidance.

First intelligence uses the *entire body* to communicate and process information. The outdated belief that intuition is strictly a right-brain intelligence, and logic a left-brain specialty, has been replaced by the understanding that every cell in our body is capable of powerful levels of intuitive communication. This invisible language of energy exists between the structures within cells, between individual cells, between the body's organs, and even between the body and the external environment. Tiny cellular information-processing units combine with others to create tissues, the tissues combine to form organs, the organs combine to form systems, and the systems combine to form a complete biological communication unit: the human body.

The majority of the intuitive power, however, is housed in the three individual intelligence systems I mentioned earlier: the brain, the gut, and the heart. All three are equally powerful and each one is necessary to the success of the whole. But each system has a specific set of skills to provide us with guidance and other information based on what our needs are at any given moment. All three of these intuitive systems are bursting with intelligence potentials that connect us to seen and unseen possibilities at all times. And while the skill sets may differ from system to system, they all have a common goal: to assist us in living at the highest possible level of survival, physically, mentally, emotionally, and spiritually.

THE BRAIN

We are told that the brain is the center of our genius. (As I will discuss a bit later, this may not actually be the case.) This part of our anatomy is made up of about three pounds of gelatinous water, fat, and protein and connects our central nervous system to every cell and interprets every signal from within and outside the boundaries of our body.

The adult human brain possesses over 100 billion neurons, which are chemically stimulated, *electrical* connections that form our habits, patterns, memories, and perceptions. These passageways of information are in a constant state of rewiring, growing, and adapting and will continue their process of microscopic combustion until the day we die. The idea that once a brain is completely developed (usually by adolescence) these patterns are permanent is steadily being proven wrong by new science.[1]

This is especially exciting in the realm of intuition, because it reveals that through will, the focus of attention, and practice, we can rewire our brains to function in new ways and can expand and alter how we perceive the world around us. This gives us a limitless capacity for growth and evolution and opens the door to new methods of creating health, happiness, abundance, or anything else.

The brain acts as a central processing unit for the five senses, using the organs of taste, touch, smell, sound, and sight as its interface, but it *isn't* the only organ of perception that provides our awareness with information. We are, in fact, *literally* covered head to toe with a sophisticated and sensitive information supercomputer: the skin.

Our External Brain

The largest organ in the body, our skin is made up of the same types of cells that make up our brain. In the earliest embryonic stages, we develop three cellular layers that create the full human organism: the ectoderm, the mesoderm, and the endoderm. The endoderm and mesoderm give rise to virtually all systems and structures in the body: muscle, blood, bone, glands, eyes, organs, and so on. The ectoderm, however, gives rise to only two: the brain, with its extended nervous system, and the skin.

Because both are sourced from the same cellular origins, the skin should be considered an extension of the brain. And just like the brain, the skin operates as an information-processing center, an interface between our consciousness and our environment.[2]

Have you walked into a dangerous place or met a creepy person and had the hair on the back of your neck or on your arms stand on end? Or conversely, have you seen a stunning sunset or been in a sacred or spiritual place and felt the same thing? It is because the skin — which we now know is literally the brain covering the body — is reacting to an energetic "something" it perceives in the environment and is communicating that information to the nervous system by giving us physical feedback. This is a powerful facet of our intuitive intelligence at work.

Small but Mighty

The final aspect of the intuitive intelligence carried in our brain is held within a tiny endocrine gland buried deep within the brain called the pineal gland. This pinecone-shaped lump of tissue is lodged between the two hemispheres of the brain and becomes visible in the fetus about forty-nine days after conception. It produces the hormones melatonin and serotonin, which affect our daily biorhythms of mood, sleep, wakefulness, hunger, and thirst, as well as other energetic functions such as sexual desire, puberty, aging, and immune functions.

While science is still unraveling the specific powers of this organ, it has recently been discovered that the pineal gland contains light-sensitive cells that function like those found in the retina of the eye, validating the idea that to a certain degree it can "see."[3] Why do you suppose it is necessary for an organ so deeply buried within the darkness of the body to be able to see? What could we be looking at in there? Could it be that we see into the realms of our inner awareness? The mystics seem to think so, which is why for millennia this gland has been called the "third eye."

The pineal gland is stimulated by certain chemical, magnetic, and electrical fields and seems to become especially active during meditation and visualization practices. These stimulations are known to cause an increase in what is commonly termed "psi," meaning psychic events, which take shape as expanded visionary ability, out-of-body experiences, lucid dreaming, and increased intuitive capacity. Subjects who have worked consistently to activate and engage their pineal gland also report having a better memory, clearer sensory perception, stronger intellect, and greater imagination. All of these are deeply powerful aspects of a highly developed intuition.

THE GUT

The second power player on the intuitive intelligence team is the enteric nervous system. It is an often overlooked but highly effective network of neurons held within our digestive tract that some scientists call our second brain. This brain in our belly is responsible for the automatic intuitive process we all know as "gut instinct," and it operates in cooperation and partnership with the brain in our head to provide us with information as a response to our external environment.

In an embryo, the enteric nervous system develops when the part of the brain known as the neural crest splits into two separate systems, becoming the central nervous system and the enteric nervous system.

The central nervous system takes care of the functions of every part of the body except for the gastrointestinal tract. The enteric nervous system operates strictly in the gastrointestinal tract, and it remains connected to the brain and central nervous system through the vagus nerve.

The latter intelligence system contains 100 million neurons, so while it has about a thousand times fewer neurons than the brain, it is still considered a brain in its own right. The enteric nervous system also makes use of more than thirty neurotransmitters, most of which are identical to the ones found in the central nervous system, such as the feel-good chemicals dopamine and serotonin. In fact, more than 90 percent of the body's serotonin lies in the gut; about 50 percent of the dopamine and over 80 percent of the immune system resides here as well.[4]

This intelligence can and does operate completely independently of the central nervous system and spinal cord, which means it can gather and process information that our eyes, ears, nose, and other sensory organs are unaware of. To a very high degree our gut has a mind of its own. This is made obvious by the fact that people who suffer spinal cord injuries that damage the central nervous system can't move their arms or legs but can still digest food. So the brain in our belly is independent of the one in our head and has access to its own form of information processing and transmission. It is, however, still activated like all other intelligence systems: by influences in the environment that we may or may not be consciously aware of.

Although its influence is far-reaching, the second brain is not the seat of any conscious thought or decision making. It is instinctual and automatic and operates in a binary fashion, which means it recognizes only two choices. As in the case of computer systems, which use only two numbers — zeros and ones — to structure information, the gut operates on a simple yes/no, good/bad binary foundation.

In response to information in the environment that the enteric system notices, it excretes a myriad of hormones and chemicals that tell the body it should prepare for a threat to the organism, or that it can relax because the coast is clear. This process is lightning quick and invisible. But when you feel it, you know it.

The Enteric System's Fight-or-Flight Response

When this system perceives danger, it instantly slows down all the functions of the organs within the viscera, which include those of digestion, assimilation, elimination, reproduction, and immune function, and it pushes blood into the large muscles of the arms and legs to prepare the body for fight or flight. Its job in the moments of perceived danger is to activate the stress response so that we are prepared to take action.

When something is unsafe or inappropriate for us, when our body is telling us to "watch out," the feelings it generates are pretty hard to miss. In the moments when our enteric nervous system is telling us "no," we may perceive a sudden surge of tension, anger, or restriction and yet have no visible or obvious external cause for it.

This darkening of energy in the body may often result in a feeling of nausea or unease, or it may feel like a tightness or heaviness in the head, chest, or solar plexus. This is the "gut instinct" communicating with the organism that is "you" through the stimulation of the myriad of neurotransmitters in your belly, preparing you to take action.

This is baseline intuition and the intelligence of your enteric nervous system working at its best. It isn't very sophisticated — that is, it won't help you find answers, solve problems, or be creative, but it *will* keep you safe. If you learn to listen to it and follow the directions it gives you, it will save your butt every time.

THE HEART

The third and most powerful part of the Trilateral Intelligence System is the heart. The fist-sized piece of flesh beating thousands of times a day, pushing blood through your body, is more than just a pump. It is also the most powerful piece of intuitive intelligence equipment you possess. And it starts doing its job almost from the moment of conception.

In an embryo, the heart develops long before the brain or any other organ or system in the body. Embryologists can measure a tiny heart flutter as early as six weeks after conception. The brain and its recognizable pattern do not appear until the tenth or eleventh week, and most of the other organs do not develop until much later than that.[5]

But even at the earliest stage of development, the little metronome in our chest is operating like a tiny orchestra conductor, keeping all the cells of our developing body organized in a coherent and persistent rhythm. The heart is the intelligence that guides the development of the entire body, keeping the rhythm of the fetus in balance so that the cells that make up a toe will go where a toe belongs, and the cells that make up a liver will go where a liver belongs. All is perfectly efficient and hugely intelligent in design.

This energetic leadership sustains us throughout our lives. Research done by the Institute of HeartMath reveals that in every moment of the day, the heart is communicating with the brain in four different ways: neurologically (through nerve impulses), biochemically (through hormones and neurotransmitters), biophysically (through pressure waves), and energetically (through electromagnetic field interactions). All these energetic pathways affect the brain's activity and, ultimately, its level of performance.[6]

HeartMath's research also reveals that the heart is capable of electromagnetic, or energetic, communication and produces the largest electromagnetic field of any of the body's organs. The institute has found that the heart possesses a *magnetic* field five thousand times stronger than, and an *electrical* field sixty times greater in amplitude than, the field generated by the brain. This field of influence communicates faster than the speed of light, can be clearly detected ten to twelve feet away from the body in all directions, and has an effect on every other biological electromagnetic force within its reach. This includes the portions of the brain that are responsible for expanded awareness and intuitive perception.

This powerful force field can be sensed by other living beings in the environment, including humans, plants, and animals. It is also evidenced in people who regularly practice generating a coherent heart state that makes them more intuitively sensitive to information in the environment and within the electromagnetic fields of other living beings around them. This sensitivity empowers them to perceive more deeply than those who do not have this skill activated.

This empowered heart state supports a greater level of deep and effective communication between individuals, groups, and teams, and it provides a broader opportunity for creative problem solving, more effective crisis management, and better group cohesion. This is probably why when we have a truly meaningful conversation with another person, one that offers an opportunity to heal, connect, and empower, we call it having a heart-to-heart.

As you can see, the heart has far more power than people may have realized, and it has massive influence over the brain and all its functions. Moreover, our brain is *not* limited to the gray matter between our ears but instead covers our entire body and fills us to the very core.

MACRO TO MICRO

An expanded awareness of these physical structures makes it clearer that these operating systems are responsible for much more than moving our blood, digesting our food, and counting our toes. But this information reveals only the superficial physical aspects of the systems. More important, they also have great intelligence hiding in their nonphysical, or spiritual, aspects, which we will get to in later chapters.

For now, simply consider looking at the systems of your body not as mere organs of biological function but as powerful organs of perception that are ready, willing, and able to guide you safely and elegantly through any aspect of your life. When you begin to relate to your body as a system of intelligence and pay attention to the ways it communicates with you, you will be rewarded with a level of calm and certainty, and with a depth of relationship to it and the world around you, that is unmatched by any external source.

CHAPTER 2

THE HIDDEN WISDOM
OF DNA

The greatest wisdom is in simplicity. It's not complex or elaborate. The real knowledge is free; it's encoded in your DNA. All you need is within you. Great teachers have said that from the beginning. Find your heart and you will find your way.

— CARLOS BARRIOS, Mayan elder and Ajq'ij of the Eagle Clan

The smallest physical aspect of our intuitive intelligence system, our DNA, is considered the building block of our very humanity. This tiny bit of information, which is more energy than matter, is invisible to the human eye, but it holds all the energetic information required to create the body, house its intelligence, and provide a point of focus for all the brilliance of the universe.

DNA is the genetic human blueprint crafted from a complex structure of molecules found in the nuclei of cells. It is overflowing with the information that determines our physical existence. The information stored in these molecules instructs the cells to make certain proteins that determine our biological traits. DNA is the physical and energetic structure of *expression*. Our stomach digests, our heart pumps, and our DNA determines how we occupy space in the world.

The energetic structure of DNA is really just a repeating pattern made up of four different parts, or bases. These four bases, known as nucleotides, are adenine (A), cytosine (C), guanine (G), and thymine (T).

Think of these parts as simply letters in the alphabet, or as toy blocks that have four different shapes, all of which can be strung together in different combinations. The combination and its repeating pattern together determine how we express ourselves in the physical and energetic domain of reality. This energetic code determines how we look, how we process information, how we respond to others and to the environment, our level of health and well-being, and how well we thrive at any given moment in time.

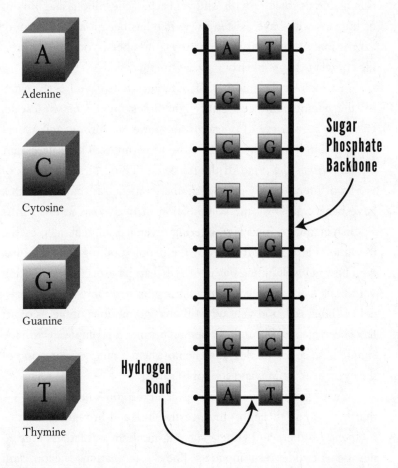

Figure 1. Our biological antenna: The structure of DNA. The building blocks on the left are strung together to create the informational code of expression.

If the coiled structure of a *single piece* of DNA were to be completely stretched out, we would have over six feet of coded intelligence. That is how much expression potential we have stored in each cell. Now multiply that by the 100 trillion cells in our body and you realize how much energetic influence we actually possess.

Every single human being who has ever appeared on the planet is a unique expression of the combination of only four building blocks. This may not seem like a large-enough variety of construction materials to work with, and yet each of the billions and billions of humans who have existed over time has been a unique form of expression. When you consider those numbers, you get a clearer idea of what is possible from a very simple code.[1]

Just look at the millions of outcomes that have been created by the combination of eighty-eight notes on the musical scale. Consider the variety of music, from Marley to Mozart and everything in between, created with those same notes. The differentiating factor was the mind of the musician. Think of the millions of works of literature — poetry, drama, comedy, adventure — that have been crafted by the combination of twenty-six letters in the English language. This is staggering diversity, all generated by the thoughts, ideas, and attitudes of the people crafting the structure. And how many stunning pieces of visual art have been created using variations from a color palette that begins with only *three* primary colors: blue, red, and yellow? Millions and millions of pieces of art have been created throughout human history, all composed with the simple base code of color, but each of them a unique expression of the eyes, heart, mind, and soul of the artist.

We too are unique expressions of all the combinations of DNA that have come through our ancestral line and brought us to this moment. Mothers and fathers shaping mothers and fathers created new genetic codes resulting in us. Those combinations of expression determine the shape our body takes, how we occupy space, and how we interact with the field of all possibility. Every expression of the past is carried within our DNA, but so too is every potential expression of the future.

Imagine that a tiny strand of molecular information is a spinning top made of light, and that all the combinations of code, even the ones that science does not yet understand, are being reflected onto the three-dimensional screen of space that is your life. Because every single cell you possess carries a strand holding the same information, all 100 trillion of your individual "conscious-cell citizens" are projecting the same story of light. The sheer volume of that energetic light show makes our reality appear solid, permanent, and very real.

But what if we could change the way our DNA expresses itself, making the light show that is the reality of our life something else entirely? It is possible. We do have the power to alter our DNA and, as a result, alter the way our biological antenna is tuned to the universal field of information.

Quantum DNA

Until recently, science characterized us as mere passengers on the ride of life who were doomed to travel a specific and preselected journey that was handed down to us from our ancestors by virtue of our genetic sequence. But work by the former CIA researcher Cleve Backster and the Institute of HeartMath reveals that our DNA, just like every cell in our body, is wildly responsive to influences within our environment and can and does alter its expression based on that information.[2]

We know that our DNA forms strands of amino acids that make up the physical and genetic structure of our bodies. The sequence of codes within our DNA strands not only indicates the size, shape, and health of our physical countenance but also determines how we process and perceive the energetic information that surrounds us, as well as how we respond to it to create our lives.

The old belief that these sequences or strands are written in stone, and that they determine the outcome of our health and happiness, all as a result of a random toss of the genetic dice, is quickly changing. The new research by Cleve Backster, Luc Montagnier, and others, which I'll discuss in a moment, now validates the idea that the power of thought and emotion is enough to permanently alter these sequences and, as a result, change how we experience the world and how it experiences us.

The quantum model of science reveals that our DNA and its various codes are in fact flashing in and out of the current moment faster than the speed of light, and that DNA actually has the ability to act as an electromagnetic communicator, or antenna. Recent research shows that DNA has the ability to send electromagnetic imprints of itself into distant cells and fluids in other parts of the body, which can then be used by the enzymes to create copies of the original DNA. This unique skill boils down to a form of biological teleportation, which suggests that our DNA is not linked to space and time.[3]

Other experiments have suggested that DNA has the ability to *discern* and *choose between* different elements according to their level of spin or frequency. This means it is attracted to energies that prove to be beneficial or are in alignment with its intent, which suggests that our DNA has a level of conscious awareness and the ability to influence what is going on around it.[4]

This evolving understanding suggests that, energetically, our DNA is a multidimensional antenna that transmits and receives information from the environment based on the frequency generated by our DNA's active code. This code is determined by the genes and proteins held in the structure of, *and* by the level of mind or intent of, the creative operator at the time. We are the creative operator. Our intent combines with the DNA's intent to connect with information in the field, and this guides us to the information we seek. This suggests that consciousness, awareness, and focused thought have a direct and powerful influence on our DNA, resulting in chemical changes in the body, which cause a restructuring of physical expression. This restructuring activates processes that can alter physical, emotional, and mental properties, which in turn influence how we perceive and interact with the environment.

To put it simply, we, as the creative artist of our life, can use our consciousness to alter and influence the moment-to-moment expression of every cell in our body, right down to our DNA. This influence empowers our DNA to directly link with the information and guidance we need and to then use it to support and sustain the new expression.

PRIMARY PERCEPTION

One of the first experiments to capture my attention concerning the cellular and energetic function of intuition and how it manifests in living organisms was the work done in the 1960s by Cleve Backster, an interrogation specialist who focused on lie detection technology.[5] As one of the pioneers in the science of truth telling, he headed one of the first training facilities that taught lie detection to law enforcement and military personnel.

Backster's most compelling discovery was the theory of what he called "primary perception," which he claimed enabled him to measure dynamic reactions from plants and other living organisms by linking them to a very sensitive lie detector and exposing them to external stimulation. He would spend the latter part of his career seeking to prove that primary perception demonstrated that an energetic interconnection exists between all living things, and that all living things have this communicative power.

Backster's investigations were not, at least at first, designed to validate the idea that plants are capable of perception of any kind. Rather, his experiments simply measured how long it took for water to reach the leaves of his dracaena cane plant when he poured the water at its base. He attached to the plant the electrodes of a polygraph machine, which normally measures the galvanic skin response (electrical reactivity) of a human being, and noticed that the plant was giving off the same sort of electrical reading that a human would.

Intrigued by this result, Backster went on to try various other methods of external stimulation on the plant, but it wasn't until he had the idea of burning the plant's leaves that his experiments really took off. Notice that I said he had the "idea" of burning the leaves; he did not actually burn them. When he thought of burning the plant, the plant immediately exhibited a powerful stress response that was clearly registered by the polygraph. There had been no physical contact with the plant in any way; the extreme reaction was based on thought alone. Backster had discovered that the plant could interpret, process, and respond to something perceived as nonphysical (thought) and could do it in such a way that it exhibited some level of rudimentary awareness of the environment.

Repeated experiments would eventually reveal something even more interesting: the plant could also tell if he was lying. When Backster initially thought about burning the leaves of the plant, he meant it and the plant responded. But when he or his assistant had the thought but only pretended they were going to take action — or to put it more scientifically, they lacked focused intention — the plant did not respond in the way it did when the intention was real.

He created similar experiments in which he observed the plant's response to the act of placing microscopic brine shrimp in boiling water. The sensitive technology of the polygraph indicated that the plant experienced measurable stress at the same time the shrimp went for their torrid swim.

It appeared to Backster that the plant was exhibiting sensory awareness and a response to an external stimulus in the physical environment; he was measuring a form of "plant telepathy." He concluded after many years of research that plants, while they do not have a nervous system and do not seem to possess any form of advanced consciousness, could perceive human intentions and were deeply sensitive to other life-forms and situations occurring in the environment around them. In later years Backster devised experiments using eggs, bacteria, and human sperm, and he claimed that primary perception was evident in all of them.

Backster's theories and practices were largely disregarded by the scientific community owing to what was perceived as a lack of repeatability. Many believed Backster had not used scientific methodology and found reason to dismiss him. Today his work is greatly appreciated by many others, who continue to advance the theory and apply it to the study of thought, awareness, and consciousness and what these mean to our well-being and to the structure of life itself.

Science, at the time of Backster's experiments, did not understand that an organism need not possess a brain and nervous system in order to have consciousness or be aware of its environment. That is changing. But more important and meaningful is a related question: if a plant has the capacity to perceive and respond to information in the environment, what are we human beings, who *do* possess a mind and a nervous system, capable of?

BREAKING NEW GROUND

In the 1990s, thirty years after Backster's experiments took place, the tools of scientific research had advanced and researchers had become more open-minded. The seed that was planted by the primary-perception studies had sprouted, and researchers advanced from studying the perceptions of plants and bacteria to studying the consciousness of the very building blocks of humanity. Nowhere is this advancement in science and consciousness exhibited more powerfully than at the Institute of HeartMath, where research on DNA and intention has shattered previous perceptions.

In a series of groundbreaking experiments, researchers isolated samples of DNA in test tubes. Each of the test tubes was given to a trained HeartMath practitioner who had highly developed skills in generating positive heartfelt emotion. The practitioners were instructed to hold the tubes for two minutes as their heart rhythms were recorded.[6] They were to have the intention of getting the strands of DNA to either wind, unwind, or stay the same. When a practitioner focused on the emotions of love, care, appreciation, and compassion, and combined that with the intention for the strand of DNA to tighten or loosen, the changes in the DNA were significant.

By holding an intention and increasing their levels of emotional coherence, participants were able to cause a change in DNA confirmation of up to 25 percent. *Confirmation* in this case meant how well the DNA held its shape, or how quickly or slowly it loosened its strands or broke its chemical bonds. These results were three times more vigorous than those produced by mechanical or thermal methods of "denaturing" the strands. (This means they got results while using the power of heart-based emotion that were three times better than they would have derived by chemically altering, heating, or shaking the living daylights out of the samples.)

One DNA sample was given to a person in the control group (which was made up of individuals not trained in heart-based emotion) who was, in fact, charged with powerful negative emotions such as frustration and anxiety. That sample produced a noticeable shift in the measurements indicating ultraviolet damage and deterioration of the DNA structure. Given the effect that this fellow's bad mood had on the sample during a two-minute trial, we can only speculate about the level of damage to *his* DNA that was happening with constant exposure to his negative state.

The crew at HeartMath was also able to use heart-based emotion to influence DNA over distances that went well beyond the field of the physical body. In a series of other experiments, the researchers increased the distance between the practitioners and the DNA samples, separating them by up to a mile. This increase in distance made no difference to the efficacy of the focused intention. The DNA responded in the same way it did when held by a practitioner.

In a third variation on this experiment, the researchers placed DNA samples in three different vials. A practitioner was asked to focus the thought of a specific outcome or intention on each of two samples, directing them to unwind to different degrees. He was asked to leave the third sample completely alone.

The results indicated that the focused intention did indeed have an effect on the two chosen samples, and that the one that was energetically "ignored" showed no change.

So What Does It All Mean?

So what conclusions are we to draw from all this information? First, Cleve Backster and his dracaena showed us that our thoughts and emotions have the ability to influence even simple life-forms, and that every living cell is in constant communication with its environment and the other living cells within it.

Second, studies by the Institute of HeartMath show us that emotions have the power to alter the structure of our DNA and, as a result, can influence how our biological antenna communicates with and processes data from the informational field. These studies also reveal that DNA is responsive to what is happening in the environment and takes action based on that information.

Third, HeartMath's studies show us that our thoughts and

emotions are nonlocal, and that we are connected to and have an effect on everything we focus on, regardless of time or space.

Fourth, HeartMath also demonstrated that we can guide and direct our thoughts and emotions intentionally toward a specific outcome, and that intention isn't a random, shapeless shot in the dark.

What do these results have to do with our biological propensity for intuitive intelligence? They reveal that we are energetically connected to everything and everyone around us, and that the power of focused consciousness has the ability to literally change matter. This ability to alter our DNA gives us the power to shape and craft our biology to serve us in ways that align with our deepest desires, and the power to use it to deliberately alter how we are physically, emotionally, mentally, and spiritually expressed in the world.

As you digest the results that these researchers and practitioners produced, keep in mind that the effects and outcomes of these experiments resulted from DNA samples that (a) did not belong to the practitioners (they were not working with their own DNA), and (b) were outside the body. If we can have an effect this powerful on DNA that isn't ours, and that isn't even inside us, imagine the effects we can have on the stuff that is ours, that is alive in us, and that we carry around with us in every cell of our body. The ramifications are simply mind-blowing!

CHAPTER 3

THE POWER OF
THE UNIFIED FIELD

All matter originates and exists only by virtue of a force.... We must assume that behind this force exists a conscious and intelligent mind. This mind is the matrix of all matter.

— MAX PLANCK

Now that we've discussed all our biological intuitive equipment, and now that you are a bit more familiar with how it communicates both physically and energetically, the next step is to link ourselves with the source of intelligence that will provide the information and guidance we seek. The questions we must ask next are: Where are we sending our thoughts when we look for intuitive information? What are we linking into when we seek guidance? In short: Who or what guides us, and where does the information come from?

THE CORE OF NATURE

Albert Einstein, who was both an avid believer in and a potent example of the power of intuitive intelligence, had a deep belief that mind and matter were unified. He theorized that there was a single field of intelligence at the foundation of everything in both seen and unseen nature. Irony aside, it was his intuition which led him to this hypothesis that ultimately would support the mystical and physical realities of how intuition works in the first place.

Modern science has validated Einstein's theory and has proven that everything we call physical reality is held within a nonmaterial field that is, at its core, a field of intelligence, or consciousness, which functions as the foundation of nature. This field, which science calls the unified field because it unites the powers of gravity, electromagnetism, radioactivity, and nuclear force, is the most concentrated source of intelligence in the universe. At its base it is not solid; it is the no-thing that contains everything. It is pure consciousness.[1]

Science calls it the unified field, but mystics throughout the ages have called it the mind of God, divine intelligence, the spirit of nature, the life principle, the kingdom of heaven, Universal Mind, the Great Spirit, the Creator, Allah, Brahma, the All, or the Father. More contemporary names for the field are *superconsciousness*, *source*, *the divine matrix*, *the universal grid*, and *the force*. The names are as varied as the languages, cultures, and belief systems that identified them, but all are alike in describing a singular powerful ground in which we all "live, breathe and have our being" (Acts 17:28 KJV).

Science has proven what the alchemists, masters, and enlightened ones have long known, that the universe is mental — that is to say, it's an environment driven by thought — and that we are swimming in a soup of nonmaterial, dynamic, and self-aware intelligence. It has also revealed that *mind* itself is the highest power *we* can use to affect, influence, and communicate with this limitless field of potential.

When we understand the mental, or conscious, nature of the universe, we can readily explain and consistently access the variety of supernormal mental phenomena, including intuition, ESP, remote viewing, and other psychic skills, that have confused people and captured public attention for centuries. With this understanding we can place intuition and other mental abilities like it back among the normal functions of everyday human biology, where it belongs.

MIND STUFF

The old ideas of science led us to believe that we were living in a universe made of inert and lifeless matter. But what we are now discovering is that the universe is instead alive, and that it is made up of the same stuff thoughts are made of. All this energetic, thoughtful stuff is a nonspecific and nonlocal field of pure subjectivity beyond time, space, and intellect.

The implications of this understanding provide us access to an incredible amount of energy, which ultimately is infinite and ever recycling itself as it is expended and returned to the field from which it came. We individualize the field through the filter of our nervous system, and what we see or experience as our reality is merely a play and display of information.

The field operates essentially as a medium that records everything, providing a means for everything to communicate with everything else. Waves encode information when they bump into one another; and because they are infinite they do not stop, so all information is held within the field and is accessible at all times. All these waves are just different ripples on an ocean of information; when one wave meets another wave of information, the interference pattern created by the connecting of the waves causes a new and isolated differentiation in the field.

To put it more simply, when a thought wave is put into the field and bumps into another thought wave within the field, it causes a new thought wave; and we notice it within the framework of our nervous system. This is how we experience an intuitive hit.

Figure 2. Wave functions interfering with one another to create a new wave function

What the study of the unified field reveals is that the material world, the things we normally perceive as physical stuff, essentially ceases to exist at the atomic level. That is, anything smaller than an atom stops being an expression or vibration of matter and, at the smallest levels, becomes an expression of intelligence.

Everything we perceive as physical is a mirage.

In the past, science assumed that consciousness and our ability to be self-aware were some sort of chemical accident, the random and coincidental outcome of the neurological and electrical processes of the brain. It was thought that because we possess a brain, we possess consciousness, and that mind itself was a function of the brain. But neuroscientists have never been able to locate the spot within the brain from which consciousness stems.

Deeper understandings have revealed that consciousness stems from every cell of the body and, deeper still, from the DNA at the core of every cell. These new understandings reveal that the qualities of consciousness are not superficial; nor do they exist as an *effect* of some other cause. Rather, because it exists as a foundation of nature, this level of consciousness, or mind, exists *as a cause*. This reveals that reality is in consciousness, not the other way around.

This foundational energy is the source of the laws of nature, which provide the orderly expression and regularity of the universe. This energy gives rise to millions of species of plants and animals and sustains the earth's ecosystems; it creates an infinity of simultaneously existing planets, solar systems, and universes and is an endlessly creative, active, and self-aware source of pure life.

THE MATHEMATICS OF LIFE

All these principles of intelligence can be revealed mathematically and are regularly used in the fields of electronics, telecommunication, aerospace, and laser technology. They give science the ability to place a man on the moon and return him home at a precise moment in time, to send a satellite into space and communicate with it from a million miles away. And, more practically, they allow us to speak to someone else on the other side of the planet and watch our favorite television show on our computer or cell phone. All the foundational elements found in this ocean of potential, which support these physical technologies, are not beyond the range of human awareness and perception. In fact, reality is as Einstein imagined: a universal ocean of possibility existing as a timeless and endless field of intelligence available to every human being in the simplest state of human awareness.

Even the scientific understanding of *empty* space, and of what empty actually means, is evolving. New discoveries reveal that an atom is 99.9999999 percent empty space, and that what was considered to be a vacuum (because nothing was perceived within it) is not empty at all but is full of, and completely embedded with, and infinitely dense with, energy. This energy is the source of everything we know, and we are saturated with it during every moment in time.[2]

We are *not* connected to it. That is, there is no imaginary cord or plug linking us to an *it* that is over there while we are over here. And we do not risk the possibility of — by virtue of being somewhere other than where *it* is — unplugging ourselves or severing the cord.

That is not possible. We are in it. It is in us. Like a marshmallow embedded in a Jell-O salad, we are covered, suspended, filled, supported, encompassed by this field of information. There is nowhere we must go to reach it or connect to it. It is in us and we are in it.

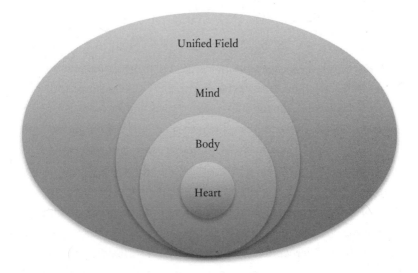

Figure 3. Our heart, mind, and body are completely encompassed by the field and the information and guidance it holds.

The creative power of the mind of nature is present in every life-form and material thing we see expressed on the screen of reality, in even the tiniest single-cell amoeba. But the amoeba is not the creative power itself.

As the creator of Macbeth, Othello, Romeo, Juliet, and countless others, William Shakespeare is the creative mind who brought all these characters to life. But the creations are not the creator. Shakespeare is present within each of his creations in that they embody a certain life force, spirit, and vitality that reflect attributes of the writer; but they are not the writer himself. This is how we exist within the creative mind of the universe. We too are created from the mind of the field of all possibilities and are heir to all its attributes and principles. We are *one* with the creative force but we are not the force itself. We are *of* God, but we are not God.

As beings who won the evolutionary lottery, we have the ability through consciousness to become aware of our one-ness with the field. And through a consistent and dedicated practice of focus we can learn to access it at will and use all its creative powers to assist us. This is what we are doing when we develop our intuitive intelligence and use it to guide us to consciously chosen higher possibilities in our lives.

Unfortunately for most of the people alive on the planet today, the erroneous collection of assumptions drilled into us by dogmatic religion, by a society hypnotized by the phenomena of matter, and by an unenlightened education system — all of which perpetuate the idea that we are separate from this field and the wisdom held within it — has become our greatest limitation and our most potent handicap.

TWO MEN IN A FIELD

Whether it be the biblical story of Cain and Abel or the modern tale of Luke Skywalker and Darth Vader in *Star Wars* or some other tale, there is a common theme running throughout all mythology that speaks to the power of an understanding of one's connection to the field. To know it is to gain power over misfortune and to take a front seat on the road to creating our destiny. To not know it is to leave our lives open to the fickle hand of fate and the dismal law of averages so readily accepted by the uninformed group mind.

Imagine that, from within the creative mind of the field of all possibility, two men are born. Both are of equal intellect and physical potential, born during the same era, and in possession of equal amounts of emotional, physical, and mental support. One of these men has an innate knowledge and complete understanding of his connection to the field of intelligence, and he is well aware of the power within him to access this field to benefit and serve him in all ways. He believes in the power of a single creative force that is the cause of all things, and he gives no external or created thing any power. That is, he gives no outside physical influence — no person, place, or circumstance — the power to determine his outcome. He knows he is *one* with the universal mind that created him, and he trusts this intelligence to guide and lead him to good fortune.

He expresses this in astounding and often miraculous ways, and his life is filled with happiness, joy, peace, purpose, and great abundance. He is a blessing to those who know him, and he is a shining example of kindness, compassion, and love. His generosity of heart inspires others to connect to their own inner greatness, and he leaves the world a far better place for having been in it.

The other man has a complete lack of understanding or knowledge of his connection to the field of creative intelligence. He believes he is alone and disconnected in the universe, and he feels he must struggle and strive to make things happen in life. His heart is filled with rage, judgment, and hate, so he strikes out at everyone and everything around him to ease his sense of bleak solitude.

He believes in the causative power of external conditions and blames them for a life that is filled with misfortune, illness, and destruction. Because of his deep pain, he takes everything for himself and destroys everyone and everything in his path in an effort to gain a sense of control and power. His legacy is one of sadness, fear, and desperation.

These two men might be Jesus and Hitler, or the Buddha and Genghis Khan, or two people no one has ever heard of. Regardless of who they are, both are born into the same field of information; and both, by virtue of their birth, are equipped with the same noble attributes and potentials. Yet one grows up to be a blessing in the world and the other grows up to be a monster. One cultivates miracles, the other destroys; one might be said to create light, the other one to create evil.

Both of these men have access to the field of all creative possibility. The sole difference is that only one knows it is there and knows how to use it.

Most of us fall somewhere in the middle between these two polarities. Perhaps we have had the opportunity to create some really wonderful things in our lives, and maybe somewhere along the line we have lost our way, gotten stuck, or created an outright disaster. I believe most of us lean toward the polarity of the light, but every once in a while many of us face situations in our lives that bring us to our knees and then knock the living daylights out of us.

Such a moment may appear in the form of an illness, a financial disaster, or a relationship blowout, or as something more soul-felt and indefinable. For example, one day we may just wake up and wonder, "What the heck am I doing here, and what does my life mean?" Moments when we are faced with this deep sense of isolation and confusion cause us to wonder if there is a way to turn things around and to question our place in the world. In such miraculous instances, the doors to true understanding loosen their hinges and prepare to blow open. It is the very power of our questioning that begins to activate our ability to discover the answer.

This universal desire to know the answers brings us to the final understanding of the unified field. The field is powerfully responsive. Embedded in this deep ocean of intelligence is an ability to respond to the thoughts impressed upon it. If you engage with it appropriately, it will reflect to you your mental projections. Without judgment, without a need to negotiate with or manipulate you, without a need for you to ask for forgiveness, it can and will respond. As a result, when we learn to direct and focus the thoughts, attitudes, and emotions we place in the field, we can be more certain that what we perceive as a result will be more pleasing and beneficial to us on our life journey.

The doorway into this limitless realm of possibility is the focused human mind. When we can reengage our connection, reactivate it, and restimulate it, we become empowered, ignited, and inspired. This is the moment when we know we are deeply embedded in and powerfully engaged with intelligence larger and more fantastic than we ever imagined. It is here, within this field of all possibility, that the fear and worry begin to vanish. This is something the masters and the mystics knew, and it has been recorded in the Bible: "The kingdom of heaven is within you" (Luke 17:20–21 KJV), "Ask and ye shall receive" (Matthew 7:7 KJV).

This field is where physics and consciousness align; it is the meeting place of science and spirit. This is where the real fun begins.

EXERCISE
DELIBERATELY ENGAGING THE FIELD

The following is one of my favorite exercises because it often surprises and amuses everyone in the class. This is a moment that completely alters most people's ideas about intuition and how it works and links them elegantly and powerfully with the ability they have always possessed to gain information from the field.

When I taught this exercise to the police, its ramifications made them a bit nervous, however, because this is the moment in the process when we move from solid material matter and begin to delve into the realm of the invisible. That realm is a place that, for the cops, held no solid evidence, and it was tricky for them to comfortably grasp.

We do need to push beyond what we may consider normal or rational if we are to gather information that is beyond normal. But you need not worry that something bizarre will happen as a result, because this is something you and I do every day.

A Simple Request

I'm going to ask you to do me a favor, however: please do not read ahead in this part without first doing the steps in the exercise in order. This is important. The entire process takes less than five minutes, so if you want to continue reading, please just skip to the next chapter, but I think you'll want to do the exercise first so you can start gaining intuitive momentum.

This exercise is fun and easy but powerful, and it will help you begin to identify your intuitive style, which is important to clarify as you move forward. But in order to gain the most benefit from it when you do it the first time, you must follow the directions without knowing about the big reveal at the end. So please do step 1 before moving on to step 2; complete step 2 before reading step 3. You get my drift?

This exercise presents an opportunity for you to become consciously aware that you deliberately engage with the unified field and to learn to identify the actions you take that enable you to do so. Throughout this exercise you will be creatively multitasking: I am going to have you strongly use the observer part of your consciousness, which will allow you to watch yourself as you are completing the exercise.

Please get yourself a piece of paper and a pen so you can write down your impressions.

Step 1

Take a moment to choose and bring up a *pleasant* memory. It can be a memory from earlier today, from a week ago, from ten years ago, or from your childhood — the timing of it isn't important. Take about fifteen seconds and lightly bring that memory to mind.

Where were you? Who was with you? What were you doing? Was it night or day? Was it winter or summer? Were you inside or outside? What feeling does this memory bring up for you? Joy? Expectation? First love?

Now quickly write those descriptive statements down on your paper. Remember, this is to be done quickly and with ease. Just jot down a few simple words or statements to describe the memory.

Step 2

Now take about sixty seconds and, with your eyes closed, relive the same memory with as much profound detail as you can. See if you can engage all your senses. Recall sights, smells, sounds, tastes, and feelings. Using the power of your imagination, engage as intimately with the memory as you can. Again, who are you with? What are they saying? What is the temperature outside? Are you eating anything? Is there a smell in the air? Is the wind blowing, or are the leaves crunching under your feet? What emotion do you feel? Make a choice to deliberately relive the experience as deeply as you can. Have fun and enjoy the process.

While you are in the memory, observe yourself during the process. What did you have to *do* in order to capture this memory? Make a mental note of what you did to shift your attention. How does your body feel? Are you calm or agitated? Is your attention focused inside your body or outside it? Are you focused on time or not? What is your heartbeat doing? Do you feel something happening in your head? If so, what?

When you feel sixty seconds has passed, open your eyes and move on to the next step.

Step 3

Now without any delay, editing, analyzing, or intellectualizing about what you have just done or about the memory itself, write the memory out in as much detail as you can. Include all the sense perceptions you noticed. If more details come to mind as you write, that is great. Write those down too. Give yourself at most two minutes for this.

Step 4

Moving on to the final step, write down what you observed about *how* you were able to capture this memory. How did you shift from present to past? What did you *do* physically? Did you move your eyes somewhere? Did you put your awareness somewhere inside or outside your body? What did you do mentally? Emotionally? There is no right or wrong answer to this question, because it is obvious that you were able to do it, so writing it down is just a way to bring the remembering process into your conscious awareness. But it's important to give this some consideration, because it is going to serve you later on in your practice.

Give yourself about sixty seconds to write down the details. Thank you.

Where Is the Memory?

Are you willing to agree that it was pretty easy to access the memory? Are you willing to recognize that remembering is something you do every day? Are you willing to state that memory and the act of retrieving it are a normal function of your mind? Unless you are afflicted with a disease or injury that inhibits this ability, the answer to these questions would be "yes."

Now here is where the fun begins. This is where the police got nervous. Please pay attention and consider this question seriously, because this is the question that shakes all the paranormal, voodoo nonsense off intuition and its ability to gather information from the unified field.

Where was your memory? Where did you have to go to retrieve it during the meditative exercise or when you were writing it down? Where was it stored? Write down your answer on your piece of paper.

Most people, many scientists included, will say the memory was stored in the subconscious portion of the brain, perhaps in the hippocampus or the frontal cortex. Okay. So let's look at that for a moment in light of what we just discussed about the unified field.

If I am to agree with you that the memory is stored in the hippocampus of the brain, then tell me what that part of the brain is made up of. Nerves and tissues, right? And what are the nerves and tissues made up of? Cells, yes? And what are the cells made up of? Atoms, right? And what are the atoms made of? Subatomic particles, right? And what are the subatomic particles made of? Energy, right? And what is the energy made of? Intelligence, information, and consciousness. And where is this intelligence?

It is held within the unified field, which, as we now know, surrounds us completely, beyond space and time, and is essentially a field of mind, consciousness, and intelligence composed of invisible waves of potential and information. Right?

So the memory itself is *not* actually held within the gross matter of your brain but is held instead in the subtle energy of the unified field. Every memory you have had or will ever have is stored within that field of intelligence for all time. Every memory ever had by any person is stored within that field for all time.

So I will ask you again: how easy was it to gain access to your memory?

If I had asked you the "real" question at the beginning of this exercise — which is: "How easy is it to use your mind to gain access and information from the unified field?" — you probably wouldn't have known how to answer that question. But the reality is that gaining intuitive information that can shape your future is just as easy as gaining information that has shaped your past. It is simply a matter of belief and of understanding the principles of mind as they relate to the field of intelligence. When I have done any sort of intuitive work, whether it is during what I call a "clarity session" for a client or while I am assisting law enforcement, the shift of mind that takes me from regular perception to expanded intuitive perception happens just as if I am remembering something. I am not projecting anything anywhere; I am not sending my thoughts out anywhere. I engage the same mental shift I use when accessing a memory, and the information I need for the moment at hand appears on the inner screen of perception.

I know that the information I need is held within me already, because of my unity with the field, so I don't have to go anywhere other than within my own mind to get it. Just as when I retrieve a memory. Becoming aware of what you do when you shift your mind to gain information, even if it is a memory, will benefit you as you move forward in your practice. Becoming really good at identifying how you do this within your own biology — physically, emotionally, and energetically

— will help you learn the language and develop the skills all the more quickly.

Ultimately, when using First Intelligence to guide you to information that will help craft your destiny, all you are doing is accessing the field to find information about something that has not happened yet. Essentially you are remembering the future, which is literally — I promise — no different from remembering the past.

I invite you to ponder this possibility for a little while. Then consider the fact that this reality applies to everything you see, sense, and experience in your life.

Wowza!

Determining Your Style

Now go back to the descriptive details you wrote down in step 3. Make a note of how many of the impressions were based in sight. How many in sound? How many in taste? How many in feeling? How many in smell?

Whatever sense you found was more active in the memory will tend to be the predominant or most active intuitive sense as you move forward. Most people find that one is dominant and one or two others are strong but not dominant. You can also determine what your intuitive style might be by considering how you best learn information in the material realm. That is, what is your cognitive learning style?

Some people learn visually, which means that in order for them to understand and integrate a certain teaching, they have to see it. Others prefer to hear it, such as through a lecture or even through music or song. Still others are kinesthetic: they need to feel it or do it in order to understand and integrate it. Even taste and smell can be dominant senses. Just ask any chef or wine expert how important these senses are to their ability to learn. No particular sense is stronger or better than any other, so do not judge or analyze yourself at this or any other stage of the process. Just notice what you notice and remind yourself to stay aware of the strength you have identified as you move forward.

What you perceive as your dominant senses may change as you improve your skills. Ideally, all of them will eventually become empowered to some degree, and you can enjoy the process of how they reveal themselves to you as you work with them. But we will discuss this in much more detail a bit later.

I hope you have enjoyed this brief journey through the field of everything that makes up our reality. It is a place you will return to over and over again to gather information, make new discoveries, and creatively craft the outcomes that will shape your future.

PART II

THE FOUNDATION OF INTUITIVE INTELLIGENCE

CHAPTER 4

PEACE

Peace. It does not mean to be in a place where there is no noise, trouble, or hard work. It means to be in the midst of those things and still be calm in your heart.

— ANONYMOUS

Now that we have pinpointed all the working parts of our First Intelligence and how they operate, our job is to start putting it to work. In order for First Intelligence to function powerfully and dependably, we must understand the energetic foundation that supports, empowers, and sustains it.

Unless we *intimately* understand this foundation, our intuition will not be stable or secure enough to stand the rigors of everyday use, never mind what might happen when things get a little chaotic. As you move forward in your practice, it's important for you to remember the principles that support your intuitive framework. They are crucial to your achieving success, and you will in time begin to use, trust, and depend on them every day, whether you are using them for intuitive work or simply to navigate normal day-to-day life.

The Intuition Triad

There are three foundational elements that you must constantly consider when you deliberately engage your intuition in order to change any aspect of your life. They are peace, precision, and perception.

Peace is the energetic starting point of, and primary source of, our intuitive action. Without peace there can be no accurate communication with the higher mind.

Precision is the awareness with which we notice the words, thoughts, emotions, and feelings we use in every moment, especially when seeking intuitive information or direction.

Perception is the process of becoming aware of what we notice or experience through our senses, as a reflection of reality, and aware of how to use it to shape our lives.

All three of these elements are equally dynamic and important to the process, but peace is where you must begin. Precision and perception are equal parts of the equation, but they do not support the structure. Without peace at the base, the other two have no power.

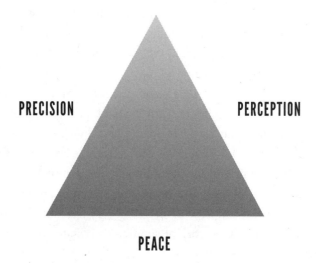

Figure 4. The intuition triad

PEACE

Be calm in your heart. This is *the* most powerful understanding you must carry with you when developing your intuitive intelligence. A calm and peaceful heart creates a calm and peaceful mind, and a calm mind is the center of all creative power.

Remember that the *mind* is the access point to the unified field of all information. Because it is the vessel through which all your alchemical transformations will pass, it is crucial that it be free of energies or patterns that distort or disrupt the possibility for you to gain the accurate guidance you seek.

The information you put *out* into the field, like the information you *get back* from the field, is shaped by the energetics of your mind. As we quiet the chatter of our lower mind and detoxify ourselves by ceasing the constant stream of often negative external stimulation, we begin to activate and amplify our intuitive connections. Think of it as clearing the grime off your windshield or clearing the static from your radio receiver: the only way to have a clear line of communication is to continually tidy up what is going on inside you.

This peace is an *active energy* that is highly vibrational and loaded with information and potential. Science calls this focal point of energy the "zero point" and considers it the "ground state or lowest energy state of any given field."[1]

The scientific belief is that if we could learn to tap this hidden point of power, the need for fossil fuel or material sources of energy of any kind would become obsolete. And just as it has the potential to power the planet, so, too, does zero-point energy have the potential to power our dreams and desires for success, happiness, and well-being.

Peace is the single most potent foundational energy in a life of mastery, and it is the energetic source of all creation. Peace is the access point for all evolutionary information that we will ever need.

Mystics and masters have known of this hidden place of power for centuries and have tried countless times to tell us about it. Most people, however, are too distracted to pay attention or too stressed-out to care.

I understand the reality that life requires us to participate in it, that there are responsibilities we must consider and work we must complete in order to survive. I am not for a moment suggesting that using our intuition to guide and direct our lives in a way that we find pleasing requires us to give up everything we have created or sacrifice the things we enjoy and move to a monastery. Quite the contrary.

Using intuitive intelligence can make what we have even better, and knowing how to create our lives from this place of peace can bring more joy to the surface; it can allow us to see and appreciate more of life's beauty and give us the freedom to truly let go of what does not serve us. There is a way to cultivate this power point, so that we can say, as the masters say, "Be *in* the world but not *of* it."

But we *do* have to cultivate that power; it doesn't just appear on its own. How do we do that?

Life According to Bob

Before I answer that question, please take a look at the image of the pendulum named "Bob."

Imagine that life, the job, the kids, the mortgage, the in-laws — and all the other stuff Bob has to deal with daily — exist in the environment that surrounds that little ball. He is relentlessly swung in all directions. Back and forth, left and right, up and down, and even in circles, all depending on the force exerting itself on him at any given moment. Bob's world is in chaos, and he is a helpless victim of things beyond his control; he is constantly tossed around at the whim of a cruel world. Maybe you can relate.

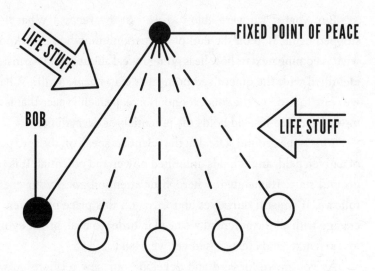

Figure 5. The pendulum of peace

Poor Bob. No peace for him, and certainly no sense of power or connection to his higher intelligence or the voice of his intuition. And yet his connection to peace is present the entire time, if Bob looks in the right place for it.

Hiding in plain sight, at the top of the pendulum, above all the chaotic motion, is the "fixed point," the position that never moves and yet is the "container" of *all* movement. Without the fixed point, the pendulum could not exist. Do you recognize it?

This is the point of peace we must shift to in order to access the power of our intuitive mind.

The pendulum represents one of the simplest, but most powerful, laws of nature, the law of rhythm, which states that everything flows and moves with the patterns of action and reaction: in and out and rise and fall. It is a fact. And if we, like most people, are in a position to identify with Bob, then we are prone to *huge* amounts of emotional turmoil and a devastating lack of peace as this potent law is expressed.

But what if we were able to *raise* our awareness? What if we stopped being Bob on the end of the pendulum, who never knows what is coming next or how he is going to feel about it, and we instead identified with the quiet fixed point that exists *above* it all? What if we were to become the solid, foundational, peaceful space that is not moved and that instead holds the potential for everything?

This is the ground state that the scientists speak of, the zero point of a given field, and it holds unlimited power and potential. It is *your* ground state. Remember: where your attention goes, your energy follows. If we still ourselves and focus on this place of power, we engage with all the potential we need in order to heal, grow, evolve, love, change, and create whatever we wish to.

As you move forward and develop your new relationship with peace, notice those moments when you identify with Bob and allow yourself to be tossed around by the rhythms of the world and by the situations that you engage in. Disengaging will require some practice, but soon you will recognize the difference, because when you are not in a position of peace it will feel awful. When you notice this happening, gently remind yourself that the *real* you is not affected by the state of things around you, and imagine yourself rising above the situation. Not in a defensive or disconnected way, but in a calm, alert manner as though you are an observer simply watching the scene as you would watch a movie. As a neutral observer you'll find it easier to guide yourself into the quiet and peaceful state of your own zero point.

From *this* place, observe or take action. Notice how different you feel, and see if you can move through the situation and maintain your sense of ease. See whether, from this place of power, you can change the dynamics of the situation and fill it with grace. When you recognize how good this state of being feels, and you make it a priority to be in it as often as possible, your intuitive ability will explode and your life will begin to change in ways that others may call miraculous.

PRACTICING PEACE

Here are some things to consider when seeking to amplify your sense of peace:

- Can you let go of your opinions about how the world and everyone and everything in it should look? Behave? Be?
- Can you forgive yourself and others for past or present perceived transgressions?
- Can you release yourself from the need to be right? Loved? Admired? Appreciated? Good?
- Can you find the purpose in where you are at this moment and simply allow it to exist without wanting it to be different?
- Can you let go of the perception that a situation you want to change is "bad"?
- Can you let go of the perception that a situation you want to create is "good"?
- Can you allow other people to have their opinions without confronting them or putting your two cents in?
- Can you be peaceful when waiting in line? While stuck in traffic? When service is slow? When service is *bad*?
- Can you peacefully allow someone else to experience difficulties or even suffering without having to take it on yourself?
- Can you let go of your judgments of right or wrong? Good or evil? Love or hate? About everything?
- Can you consider other situations that cause you to feel anything but peaceful and discover a way to allow them simply to be what they are at any given time?

- Can you see that all situations are merely reflections of levels of consciousness, and that all people are doing the best they can, according to their level of consciousness?

When we judge anything, whether good or bad, we immediately knock ourselves out of the neutral position that peace requires us to occupy. My intuition shuts down completely if I formulate *any* opinion about a situation, regardless of how tragic or disturbing it may be. I cannot be sad or worried that a child is missing, nor can I judge or feel ill will toward the person who might have abducted the child. I cannot judge a criminal as bad or evil if I want to get precise information on a crime scene. I cannot feel frustrated with a client who comes to me with the same problem again and again no matter how many times we may have worked on it. I cannot let my fear that what I see may be deemed traumatic or personal keep me from telling someone about it. I must remain as peaceful as possible, or the intuitive information I receive will be distorted by the energetic field of my opinions and judgments.

In the rest of my life, when I am just being me, I cry at apple juice commercials. But when I am using my intuition for anything, all emotion has to go. Having an opinion about *anything* disrupts your peace. You can keep your opinions and give up your peace, and life will go on exactly as it always has. Or you can let go of your opinions and believe that all is well and life will unfold in ways beyond your wildest dreams. It is, as always, your choice.

A New Word for Peace

Science speaks of peace using the term *coherence*, and while these two names may differ, mystics declare peace — and biologists declare coherence — to be a function of the heart. Researchers at the Institute of HeartMath in Northern California are trailblazers in this new understanding of the intuitive power of the heart and its ability to guide us to better health, relationships, communities, and global connections.

HeartMath defines the term *coherence* as "the quality of being logically integrated, consistent and intelligible" and further describes it as "a logical, orderly and esthetically consistent relationship of parts."[2] Coherence indicates connectedness, cooperation, and holistic balance in a system that has many individual moving components, all of which are synchronized so that the whole is greater than the sum of its parts.

As we discussed previously, the body is made up of several intuitive systems. A sustained level of coherence (peace) causes all the parts to produce together a dynamic and evolutionary field of energy that allows us to use our power of will and focus to cultivate and create brand-new outcomes and opportunities for our lives. This energy is the entry vehicle we will use to gain access to the unified field, and through which all our intuitive information will flow.

This coherent teamwork can be likened to that of a symphony orchestra. All the individual instruments do their own thing, but the focused direction of the conductor keeps them playing in tune with one another. The conductor is the source of coherence for the orchestra. Our heart is the source of coherence for our intuitive biology. The more peaceful and balanced the energy of the heart, the more peaceful and balanced the energy of the entire human system — body, mind, and spirit.

THE LANGUAGE OF THE HEART

The field of coherence generated by a heart focused on feelings of well-being, appreciation, gratefulness, compassion, and care organizes all frequencies of the body in what is known as entrainment. The greater the amplitude of this coherence, the greater the degree of relatedness, cooperation, communication, and harmony. To put it simply, when a body is supported in a field of coherence, all members of that biological community begin speaking a common energetic language and can more effectively work together to achieve a common evolutionary goal.[3]

Coherence aligns all the biological systems, and whether we are tiny embryos or mature individuals with 100 trillion cells, coherence allows us to move ahead elegantly and efficiently without a single conscious thought. Digestion, immune function, cell repair, oxygen transport, hair growth, problem solving, creativity, and idea generation all happen without a moment's pause.

Fear, worry, anxiety, frustration, and anger are examples of negative emotions that generate incoherent patterns in the heart. This incoherence causes the different players in the body to play their own tune and speak their own language, which disrupts connection and balance between the individual parts. When the energetic fields are incoherent, or what we might more commonly call *stressed-out*, the detrimental effects on our bodily functions are vast and far-reaching.

STRESS/INCOHERENCE

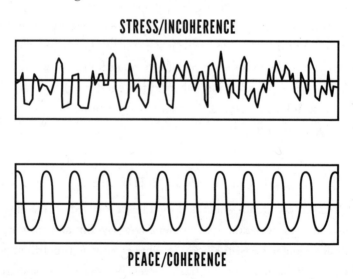

PEACE/COHERENCE

Figure 6. The incoherent/coherent heart

The diagram showing stressed and incoherent heart rhythms, as opposed to peaceful and coherent heart rhythms, clearly illustrates what happens in the intuitive system when we do not embody a foundation of peace. We don't even need to know the science behind the images; simply looking at the jagged, distorted lines of the incoherent heartbeat, or the smooth, balanced lines of the coherent heart, is enough to create a certain feeling within the body.

Take a moment to look at the two different images. As you look at the top image, think of an instance when your thoughts, feelings, or emotions made your heart beat that way. Then look at the bottom image and bring to mind the thoughts or emotions that made you feel *that* way. Do you notice a difference between what happens in your body when you look at one image and what happens when you see the other? No doubt you do.

On a subtle level these images influence your level of coherence, because, as noted earlier, the body responds to *everything* in the environment. Even an image of incoherence can cause us to feel incoherent. This is why beautiful art or a stunning moment in nature moves and inspires us, and why images depicting anger or ugliness diminish our sense of well-being.

When we deliberately and intentionally focus our awareness on genuine, positive, heartfelt emotion, we alter every biological function in our body, including the functions of our intuitive intelligence. When we amplify coherence, we regain access to the life-affirming intelligence connected to growth and evolution. The refined skills of the higher mind, which include imagination, innovation, and inspiration, once again have room to maneuver, and we move into the state of being that is commonly called "the zone" — the source of continuous, agile creativity and inspired action.

For a simple example of the power of coherence, compare the efficiency of a forty-watt lightbulb and that of a laser beam. Did you know that it takes just as much energy to power a forty-watt bulb in your living room as it does to energize a laser beam reaching from the earth to the moon? There is no trick of language here; the same amount of energy powers each, yet one is far more efficient.

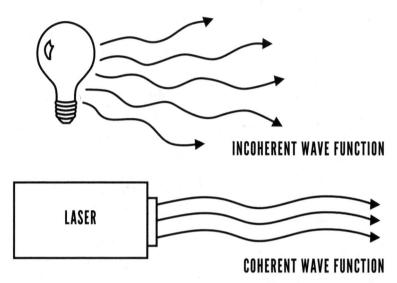

Figure 7. Incoherent bulb vs. coherent laser

The laser beam has a *coherent* wave measurement: all its energy is aligned in a constant and steady phase. Because of this coherent flow, it wastes less energy than the lightbulb does, and forty watts enables it to project farther, faster, and more precisely.

The incoherent energy of the lightbulb makes its light diffuse and weak, just as incoherence within our own systems makes us diffuse and weak. The coherent energy of the laser beam makes it precise and powerful, which is exactly what we want from our intuitive intelligence.

CLEARING THE STATIC

To build a foundation of peace, we must understand the situations, ideas, and attitudes that shift us out of coherence and create distortion or static on our intuitive line. These situations are fields of energy that influence us every moment of our lives, and they exist both externally and internally. Externally they can be generated by the conversation we had with our boss, client, child, or spouse; the movie or television shows we watch; and the invisible transmission of our cell phones and wireless Internet devices.

Internally, they are generated from moment to moment by what we are thinking about, and by the beliefs, habits, patterns, worries, and ponderings we carry. And because we are all transmitters *and* receivers of information, we are not only putting our own patterns out into the environment but picking up everyone else's as well.

We have little or no control over the energetic information that we are exposed to externally, but we do have control over our internal fields of information, *if* we know how to identify them. Once we identify the sources of our internal disruption, we can eliminate them and reopen the clear channel through which intuitive intelligence flows.

The five main causes of intuitive static are as follows.

Stress or Fear

When we experience stress and fear, the rhythms of the heart and brain shift into erratic patterns that make access to the higher mind impossible. We must be certain that our patterns of emotion are as neutral as possible, and that we do not invest too much in either positivity or negativity.

Preconceived Ideas

If you think you have all the answers, believing there is only one solution to a problem, or that there is no solution, then intuition's pathway becomes constricted. People who know it all have little access to intuitive intelligence, because their minds tell them, "I know there is no other solution than mine, so why bother looking for it?" And people who believe there is no solution at all shut the same door.

The mind must be completely open to all possible solutions or ideas. We must also be willing to let go of the need to know how intuitive information will make itself known to us or what the successful outcome will be.

Alcohol or Drugs

Anything that distorts a person's ability to function or focus on *any* level will create resistance on the intuitive channel; even extreme amounts of caffeine or sugar can cause static. Excessive exposure to computer games, loud music, violent media, the Internet, and cell phones is "artificial stimulation." Anything that interferes with our natural coherence should be kept to a minimum to ensure that our intuitive instrument is as healthy as possible.

Wishful Thinking

Having a deep desire or wish for something to turn out a certain way amps up the incoherence of our heart and brain patterns. When we are strongly attached to how something is supposed to work out, or panicked about achieving a specific result, we stand a greater chance of misinterpreting messages from our lower mind as intuitive direction.

When we trust in the process of First Intelligence and have faith that our higher mind will present us with a more expanded view of the situation, we can let go of our need to control the outcome.

Not Believing You Are Already Intuitive

Everybody is intuitive; it is a natural, biological process. We need not be gifted to have access to this powerful tool. However, we live in a world that favors the logical, rational mind, so anything that falls outside this norm is perceived as supernatural or unrealistic. Fear of, and advance judgment of, what until now has been "the unknown" prevents us from even trying to access our intuitive intelligence. Believe that you already possess this intelligence, and that it is a completely normal part of your humanity.

Before you engage in any sort of intuitive inquiry, do a quick check of your coherence level. If you notice that you are feeling anything other than peaceful, take a few minutes to establish the necessary field of energy. The extra time you take to establish this foundation is a small price to pay to ensure your intuitive success and overall well-being.

CHAPTER 5

PRECISION

He who walks straight, rarely falls.

— LEONARDO DA VINCI

The second *p* in the peace-precision-perception triad, precision plays the strongest role in how we effectively and consistently recognize the voice of our higher wisdom. This precision is reflected not only in our ability to become deeply intimate with how our body and mind use intuition but also in our understanding of the ways that it manifests itself in order to guide us both physically and spiritually to our highest good. It is an essential starting point.

Precision must be part of every aspect of our intuitive practice. Think of it as similar to the work done by a diamond cutter who cuts away whatever blocks the brilliant light within the raw stone. The steady hand of the craftsman, committed to precision, removes the rough edges that scatter the light, allowing the beauty deep within the gem to shine.

Precision shapes the energy that becomes our intuitive conversation; it shapes the results we seek, the actions we take, and the outcomes we achieve. Precision is the aspect of the intuition triad that requires the most personal responsibility from us.

JUST TO BE PRECISE

Precision is *not* the same as perfection.

Perfection is an idea of subjective limitation. Perfect according to whom? Perfect according to what? Perfection cannot be applied to a mathematical principle.

Precision is an aspect of objective measure. If we are precise in our measurements, we know what time the sun will rise tomorrow, we know what size shoes to buy, and we know that $4 + 4 = 8$.

Think of the intuitive process as a mathematical equation, a simple formula that provides you with an answer or an outcome. There is no sentimentality to this formula; it does not judge or favor anyone. It operates simply on the mathematical principle that what you put into something equals what you get out of it.

We are precise when we are very specific about the thoughts, words, emotions, and attitudes we bring to the intuitive formula. This formula should be approached not neurotically but rather with focused ease. We should simply be aware that there is a formula, and that if we expect to use it to gain a certain level of success, we will be well served if we follow that formula.

Precision allows us to be clear about the subtle yet powerful differences in the minutiae of language, thought, feeling, expression, and interpretation that are crucial to our intuitive success. Precision is expressed through recognizing and acknowledging levels of energy — mental, physical, or emotional — that could be categorized as distorted. Because the language of intuition is *so* subtle, it is crucial to discern the difference between the beneficial impulses that will lead us to appropriate information, and the distorted impulses that will cause us difficulty.

We must look deeply and compassionately into what is stored in our own heart and mind and, with a gracious lack of sentimentality, be willing to go through all the energetic clutter we have stored in there. We must honestly look at what we really need to let go of and what is all right to hold on to. Intuition serves us more powerfully when both the closet of our past and the hope chest for the future are empty. This is not meant to suggest that we let go of our desires and dreams for what is to come, but only that we let go of the limited ideas of how we expect them to show up for us.

Precision requires us to ask, "What is the foundational energy on which I have built and am living my life?" and to have the courage, grace, and willingness to be honest enough to identify it without judging or demeaning ourselves in the process. It requires us to ask, "How *clear* am I at this moment? And am I holding on to anything energetically, emotionally, mentally, or physically that has the power to distort my clear line of communication?"

It requires that we ask ourselves, "How am I entering this intuitive conversation? Do I have any malice, any unaddressed feelings of victimization or unworthiness? Or am I entering the gate of understanding with a sense of peace, confidence, and total self-acceptance?"

Precision Aspect 1. What Do You Want? (Intention)

The first aspect of precision to consider is the question we choose to seek an answer for. We must be clear about the goal we want to achieve. We want to heal ourselves. We want to solve a financial problem. We want to find a solution to a crisis at work. We want to communicate better with our teenager. We want to lose twenty pounds. We want to develop a career that supports us financially and rewards us spiritually. The endgame can be anything we want it to be, but we have to be clear about what it is.

Considerations: The important thing to become clear about first is: what is your intention here? What do you want your intuitive intelligence to guide you toward? Then you can ask yourself as many questions as you wish to help you gain even greater clarity. Some of these clarifying questions might be: What do I want to create? What do I want to solve? What do I want to heal? What do I want to become? Where do I want to live? How do I want to spend my time? What is my vision of happiness? What would create joy and ease for me?

Precision Aspect 2. What Are You Adding to the Equation?

The second aspect of the equation is the precise understanding of the energies, words, thoughts, and attitudes we use in order to get the appropriate response. We cannot enter the intuitive conversation from a place of fear or anxiety and expect to get accurate results. If we expect to use the equation to produce the number 8, we cannot add 6 plus 5. It's nothing personal; it's principle.

Having a clear understanding of what certain emotions feel like to you, and how they make themselves known in your body, will make all the difference in your intuitive success. The ability to distinguish fearful emotions and past programming, which come from your lower mind — from emotions that stem from the wisdom of your intuitive intelligence via the higher mind — is the key to your ability to follow guidance without any resistance or uncertainty.

Considerations: Am I in a place of peace? Am I coherent? Am I afraid? Am I trying to manipulate the situation? Why am I making this choice? Am I judging? What am I trying to prove? Is there something I am trying to avoid?

Precision Aspect 3. What Do You Notice about What You Get Back?

The practice of precision does not end when we finish *our* part of the conversation. It continues as we begin to perceive the information that is supplied to us from the field.

The ways we perceive intuitive information are varied and are unique to each of us. (We will discuss precisely what those variations are in a later chapter.) Having the ability to instantly recognize the feel or sensation produced by that information, and to place it in the category of truth or distortion, allows you to immediately know if your impressions are originating in your higher mind or are coming from fear, wishful thinking, or ego. With practice and attention to detail, eventually we become fluent in the energetic language our intuition speaks, and the conversation we have with it flows easily and effortlessly every time.

Considerations: How do the impressions I am perceiving make me feel? Is this information aligned with truth? With distortion? Am I clear about my perception of the difference between the two?

EXERCISE
AN INTUITION TASTE TEST

One of the most common questions I get when teaching people how to use their First Intelligence is: "How do I know when it is my intuition directing me, and when it is my fear or my ego or something else?"

The first way to gain greater certainty is to be precise about whether you have started the intuitive conversation from a foundation of peace or not. If you are asking for guidance from a place of anxiety, fear, or worry, you can be 100 percent certain that the information you perceive is not from your higher intelligence.

The next step in determining what your First Intelligence *does* feel like is to become crystal clear about what it *doesn't* feel like.

Imagine this exercise is like a thirty-two-flavor ice-cream taste test. You are blindfolded, and you have all the flavors in front of you: chocolate, mint, pistachio, rocky road, strawberry cheesecake, and all the rest. Your mission is to find the vanilla among them. But to know vanilla, you will have to have tasted it at least once before.

Take a moment and do what you can to recall the feelings and impressions of past intuitive experiences — when you thought, just maybe, your First Intelligence was communicating with you. Whether you listened to it or not, you have an idea of what it felt like. Be clear and specific about how that impression *felt* in your body. Become intimate with it and describe it precisely, as if it were a flavor of ice cream. Then acknowledge the feeling to yourself, saying, "This is my intuition; this is what truth feels like."

Then realize that all the other feelings, emotions, and thoughts that are *not* expressions of your intuitive intelligence also are specific feelings and impressions. I call these the polar opposites of intuition distortions. The distortion of fear, for example, is a certain flavor; it feels a certain way in your body — in your gut, your head, and your heart. Recall a time when you know you were fearful. Get very familiar with what fear feels like in you. Identify it. Describe it.

The distortion of paranoia has a different flavor. Recall a time when you know you were being paranoid. Re-create that feeling in your body. Get clear with what it feels like to you. Identify it. Describe it.

Manipulation has a flavor, as do arrogance, selfishness, and jealously; so do love, compassion, and generosity. Become intimately familiar with all these aspects of yourself. Only by becoming intimate with *yourself* can you learn to tell the difference between the thoughts and feelings that stem from the distortions of your wounded ego and the clear instructions coming from your higher mind.

As you go through the list of words on the next page and review each one, take a clearing breath, close your eyes, and notice the impressions, feelings, and sensations that occur. Do not *think* about the word; *feel* how your body responds when you say it to yourself. You may notice colors or temperatures, or hear words, or see pictures in your mind's eye. All these sensory perceptions are valid; acknowledge them and write down every impression you get.

My Precision Points

I have become so intimate with the difference between personal truth and distortion that I can tell in a heartbeat when I am getting appropriate or inappropriate information, and when my own projections are getting in the way of clarity. Your own response may not be the same as mine, but your impressions will be correct for you. There are no right or wrong answers.

This is what *truth* feels like to me: solid, stable, calm, open, clear, and potent. White is the color I sense when I perceive it. My body feels like it is bolted to the floor with a pillar running from the top of my head through to the bottom of my feet.

This is what *distortion* feels like to me: pinched, low to the ground, hollow, dizzy, and unfocused. The color: snot green. Distortion feels like tightness in my chest.

This is what *Yes* feels like to me: clean, easy. Its color: bright green, like a traffic light. When I think of *yes*, my body leans forward and my head feels open, like I have just inhaled eucalyptus.

This is what *No* feels like to me: rigid, tentative, cautious. It has no apparent color. It feels like a pressure behind my eyes, a slight queasiness in my belly.

Please go through this list of words and, using pen and paper, write down the feelings that come up as you say each word. Use short, simple descriptions, and trust your first impressions — do not second-guess yourself. Relax and have a bit of fun with it.

Yes
No
Love
Hate
Safe
Unsafe
Lack
Abundance
Fear
Certainty
Truth
Distortion

Can you discover any other polarities of your own that will further assist you in becoming more precise in your awareness?

The more specific and aware you become about the things you say, think, consider, feel, or believe, the more powerful and accurate you will become at sending and receiving intuitive information.

In time, your precision will become second nature. And because of your dedication and commitment to its practice, you will have cleared away all the obstacles to your intuitive success.

CHAPTER 6

PERCEPTION

If the doors of perception were cleansed, everything would appear to man as it is. Infinite.

— WILLIAM BLAKE

The third facet of the foundation of intuitive intelligence is perception, which is defined as the ability to see, hear, or become aware of something through the senses.

Perception is the interface between our biology and the environment; it is the conscious awareness of our external world as it is experienced through our physical senses. Perception begins even before we are born. It occupies a powerful position in our lives because it influences every action we take so that we can more readily fit into our environment. In this way, it helps to ensure our survival.

Physical perception includes the five bodily senses: touch, smell, sight, taste, and sound. It also involves the senses that allow us to be aware of our body as it occupies space, and to be aware of movement within a given environment.

Perception is common to every living organism, from microscopic to macroscopic. In simple life-forms, it influences the automatic actions that shape reproduction, respiration, digestion, and immune function; and in more advanced life-forms, it has evolved to influence the actions that shape relationships, prosperity, success, and well-being. When we stop to look more closely at these functions, we recognize that even the smallest cell, in its quest for the highest level of survival, desires all those seemingly advanced things as well.

Consider all the things you consciously perceive at any given moment. The sensation of the sun on your face, the sound of traffic through the window, the smell of your coffee in the morning, and the sight of a bird flying past your window. Every one of these sensory experiences defines how you experience, participate in, and take action in your life. This process is continuous and largely unconscious and automatic; we do not have to stop and think about how we perceive. We just do it.

The Phases of Perception

There are three phases involved in the process of perception, and whether you are using it to experience something as mundane as a car traveling past you or something as mystical as an intuitive bit of precognition, the process is the same. The three phases of perception are awareness, recognition, and action.

When we navigate through our everyday life experiences, we flash through the process without thought. But when we adapt it to serve our First Intelligence, it is important to understand the mechanics of it so we can be certain to empower our intuition in the most potent way possible.

Phase 1. Awareness

The process of perception begins when something in the environment gets our attention. The energetic information that lets us "notice" — whether it's the light reflected from a balloon into our eyes, the frequency of Mozart as it hits our ears, or the smell of a hot-dog stand registered by our nose — is at this point simply information in the field of possibility that has bumped into our sensory organs. It has not yet been processed by the mind, so it has no meaning or reality.

Once the energetic impression has been received by the sensory organ, it is translated into electrical signals that flow through the nervous system and into the brain and body to be interpreted. The actual moment of perception is when our body has gone through the lightning-quick processes of receiving and transmitting the electrical information, and not a moment before.

But awareness isn't the complete picture. We are *aware* of many, many things as they blur in and out of our present moment of reality, but not every single one of them is something we need to isolate or process.

We perceive only a tiny percentage of the millions of energetic impulses happening around us each second. The things we *do* notice tend to be the things that align with our level of consciousness, that are equal to the beliefs we have about the world and our place in it, and that are relevant to our well-being and survival. The rest gets filtered out — either it's ignored or it doesn't even register.

Phase 2. Recognition

There is much we *are* aware of, but mere awareness isn't enough to affect our physical processes. For awareness to have any impact, our brain must interpret what we are experiencing so we can give it meaning. This allows us to categorize and understand the world around us, which puts us in a better position to respond to it.

This part of the process is better known as recognition, which literally means to show awareness of, to acknowledge or appreciate. At the moment of recognition our brain identifies the stimulus and then categorizes it as, say, a rose or a hot dog, a fish or a bird, dangerous or safe, life affirming or life denying. The category or meaning we assign to that stimulus determines how or if we take action.

Phase 3. Action

The actions you take in response to the meaning you have created may be conscious, like jumping out of the way of a moving car, or unconscious, like scrunching up your face when you bite into a lemon. They may be major, like slamming on the brakes to avoid hitting a pedestrian, or subtle, like waving an insect away from your face. They may be life advancing, like introducing yourself to an important person you meet at a dinner party, or life denying, like staying in a relationship you know is not healthy for you. Regardless of the impulse or impression received, an action is always the final piece of the perceptive puzzle, even when the action is taking no action.

To simplify this even further, the process of perception is: What did you notice? What did it mean to you? And what action did you take? Misperceptions can threaten survival, and accurate perceptions encourage success, so these three questions hold great value for you as you develop your intuitive intelligence.

EXPANDING THE SENSES

While the biological function of *how* we perceive is pretty much automatic and beyond our control, the ability to determine *what* we perceive is entirely within our control, if we know how.

Life has *everything* in it. Everything we need to be healthy, happy, wealthy, and wise is available in the field of all possibility; nothing has been left out of this spectacular creation. It is *we* who have trained ourselves in a way that prevents us from recognizing solutions.

Beliefs, judgments, preconceived ideas, attitudes, and prejudices are distortions in the lens of our clear perception. They fog up our view and interfere with our ability to experience the beneficial opportunities available to us that could assist us on our journey. These distortions must be neutralized so our perception can remain clear.

Focused coherence (peace) and clear intention (precision) are the elevated energies that allow us to generate accurate, powerful, and life-affirming perceptions. These elevated energies have the power to alter and even eliminate the lower, denser energies that narrow our perception and cause static on our intuitive line.

Through focus and attention we must provide our mind and body with information that is in proper alignment with what we wish to see or experience as an improved outcome. In order to perceive the world in a different way, we must give our intelligence system a new map to follow.

AWARENESS FOLLOWS ATTENTION

Have you ever made a decision to buy a new car and then, suddenly, begun to notice cars just like it everywhere you looked? That is the power of perception at work. Or have you noticed that when you're in a bad mood nothing seems to go right, that you're constantly finding something to be aggravated about?

Or conversely, when you're in love — with a new partner, a new puppy, or life in general — things look brighter, the people around you are happier, and everything seems to go better in your world. That's another example of your perception following your energetic direction.

A simple, common, but profound example of how perception works to hinder or serve us is what happens when we find ourselves in a hurry and we've misplaced our keys. We run around the house in a lather, saying to anyone who will listen, "I can't find my keys.

Where are my keys? I've lost my keys!" We spin in circles, going back through the same motions over and over again with no success.

Then someone enters the room who is not an energetic part of our discussion, and she points out the keys in two seconds flat, right there in the middle of our frenzied search zone. That person does not have the limitation on perception that we have created with the language we have been speaking both verbally and energetically.

In order to perceive the things in our environment that will guide us to inspired action, we need to change how we engage with the environment. *How we occupy energetic space determines what we perceive in energetic space.* This energetic occupation is constantly and continuously influenced by our attitudes, thoughts, and beliefs. To be sure that our intuitive lenses are as clear as possible, we need to be aware of what those attitudes, thoughts, and beliefs are.

SHAPING OUR PERCEPTIONS

Who were you before you had any beliefs? Do you know? Can you remember? Chances are pretty good that you can't, because we start developing beliefs at a very young age. But there is a small window of time when we are very young that our "slate" is clean, when we exist in the world belief-free, perspective-free, as perfect all-natural beings.

While very young children, we are as close to our intuitive true nature as we will ever be. As we grow, the development of the concepts *I, me, mine* and *you* and *yours*, and the recognition of separateness that reveals all the things in the physical world that are not "me," remove us from the boundless realm that, before we were born, we knew our immortal world to be.

The change from our expansive true nature to our limited acquired one happens under the radar. It takes place one incident, one statement, one perception at a time. Our innate power is covered over with fear and doubt and we become a new, limited version of our once-potent self. It happens to all of us, but few of us have been aware of this, until now.

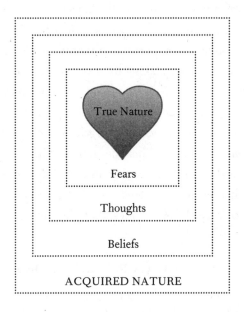

Figure 8. True nature obscured by acquired nature

That beautiful ability of young children to just *be* is eventually replaced by doing, thinking, judging, and all the other things we learn to do as we grow older. To exist in that environment we must adapt to the things that are "reality" there. The belief system and the energy that is attached to it become our normal; they become what we recognize and what is familiar. They form the energetic lens through which we perceive and experience everything in the world around us. As we grow and begin to develop lives of our own, we continue to perceive the world as we have been taught to; we find ourselves existing in circumstances, relationships, and environments that feel normal. We create a life that aligns with that energy, whether it is something we consciously want or not.

THE ENERGY OF IT ALL

Every thought, belief, attitude, and emotion is a small piece of energy that creates an energetic impulse with the ability to clarify or distort how we perceive the world. These energetic distortions envelop us in a continually vibrating cocoon. They determine the choices we make that empower us to create happiness or chaos, health or disease, and abundance or poverty. Because we are intuitive beings, those ever-prevalent energies permeate every part of our awareness. The energies of our adopted beliefs become our new nature. This new nature tells us if we are smart or stupid, attractive or ugly, worthy or unworthy, loved or unloved, and is continually reflected in our personal choices, anxieties, health, finances, and relationships.

This false nature is the energetic block of ice that must be melted in order for our intuitive intelligence to serve us. The truth of the matter is, we do not even need to know or specifically identify the beliefs and distortions we carry; we need only acknowledge that we have them. Acknowledging the fact that they exist, and knowing that they are not really who we are, diminishes the majority of their power. The rest of the cleanup job happens when we break their energetic hold on us by understanding the elevated energies of coherence and intention and applying them.

Even though these distortions may have caused us pain and frustration and limited us in the past, we must not judge them to be negative, wrong, bad, or evil, because to judge one aspect of the self is to judge the whole self. And this judgment, no matter where it is projected, will limit our ability to accurately perceive. Judgment of any kind disrupts and distorts the frequency of coherent, peaceful energy needed to access the field.

Instead of shunning these energetic distortions that have, until now, caused us to experience lack and limitation, we must, through the focused power of a coherent and peaceful heart, use them to guide us to greatness. Through this practical yet mystical function, it becomes possible to achieve true and clear intuitive perception.

THE LAW OF POLARITY

Inherent in every energetic structure, whether that structure is an amoeba, a relationship, a human body, or a life circumstance, there exists a mystical and scientific principle known as polarity. This principle states that in everything, there are two poles, or opposite aspects, that are really just two sides of the same thing. What lies between them varies by degrees. Moreover, everything in existence is dual in nature.

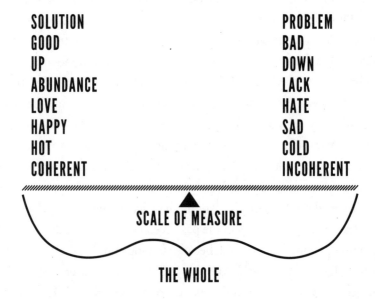

SOLUTION	PROBLEM
GOOD	BAD
UP	DOWN
ABUNDANCE	LACK
LOVE	HATE
HAPPY	SAD
HOT	COLD
COHERENT	INCOHERENT

SCALE OF MEASURE

THE WHOLE

Figure 9. The principle of polarity

Heat and cold, while opposites, are just different versions of the same thing. They are both measures of temperature; they differ only in degree. Up and down. Light and dark. Noise and quiet. Hardness and softness. Masculinity and femininity. Positivity and negativity. Even love and hate. All of them are simply varying degrees of a particular phenomenon. Can you tell with any certainty where, on a scale, either begins or ends? Where does hot begin and cold cease? When is it officially, totally dark, and when is it really light? When exactly do we move from liking someone to loving her? Or hating her?

This truth exists within our lives as well and plays out in the dynamics of lack and abundance, disease and wellness, struggle and ease, and success and failure, among other polarities. There is no absolute; there are only variations in levels of vibration. One cannot have one aspect without the other.

Why is this important for us to understand? Because when we reject or despise *any* part of our lives, we reject and despise the whole. If we focus on the perceived darkness in ourselves with resentment, shame, or anger, we send that emotional energy into *all* aspects of our existence. It cannot *not* be so.

When you are able to understand these aspects and appreciate, even a little, how they may have served you, you unleash a torrent of energy that was once used to hold the negative perceptions in place. This release is like opening the floodgates on a dam that has held water back for eons. Instead of sitting still and stagnating, this energy can now be used to bless and empower your life.

Look through your life and see where you are wasting energy by "cursing the darkness." Can you open your heart and broaden your perception enough to instead see the light within it? Can you acknowledge why these moments may have been necessary as part of your evolution? If you can, your life will begin to broaden and expand in ways you may not have believed possible.

When you adopt a wider perspective, you automatically step out of patterns of learned helplessness and release the limitless potential of the energy in your soul and become a cocreator with the universe.

At the earliest stages of this shift in perception, the illusions that once blinded us begin to lose their charm and glamour. The truth, when revealed, can sometimes be a tough pill to swallow, and life for a time may become a bit unbalanced. But if you stay dedicated to your practice, this phase will be short-lived, and you will begin to experience the positive results of your efforts. The more elevated ideas of the higher mind, including the ideas and solutions you need, will begin to appear through your now-crystal-clear lens of perception.

Expanded perception becomes a part of daily, waking consciousness and expresses itself more and more as direct knowledge and powerful wisdom. As we step nearer to our goal, we realize it is not the world that has been altered; it is we who have changed. The person we used to be, who believed in ideas of limitation and lack, has been chipped away to reveal the person we have intentionally chosen to become. We understand now that the beauty and possibility of our lives has always been there, waiting for us to discover it.

EXERCISE
EXPANDING PERCEPTION

The purpose of this exercise is to perceive things in the environment exactly as they are, and to be aware of everything that is happening, both inside and outside, at any given moment. This exercise will help you learn to direct your attention to a specific area of your body, or to a person, place, or thing in your local or nonlocal environment, and to notice what you notice when you engage with that particular field of energy. As with all exercises, it is important to start from your foundation of coherent peace.

It may be helpful for you to read this process aloud and record it, so you have a verbal guide to assist you through the process whenever you want to practice it. Or you can download it from my website, www.simonewright.com. Relax, enjoy the journey, and let your powers of imagination and visualization soar.

Let's take a trip. Get into a comfortable seated position. Close your eyes. Take a few deep, cleansing breaths and cultivate your field of peace through the heartfelt energy of coherence.

Heart

Focus now on the space around your heart. With specific intention, send your awareness to the space behind your breastbone. If it helps to place your hand over your heart, then feel free to do so. Take a few moments to generate in your mind and heart the feeling of love, appreciation, care, satisfaction, or gratitude. Choose any feeling that you feel most connected to, and allow the sensation of that feeling to fill your entire body.

Imagine that your heart is encompassed by a cocoon or bubble of energy. Take a few deep breaths while focusing on this space, and notice what you notice. Can you hear your heart beat? Is there anything special about the feeling or vibration you notice? Engage with this energy as much as possible, and when you have spent a few moments here, ask your heart, "Is there anything I need to know at this time?"

What, if anything, do you perceive? If you do receive something, acknowledge the information with a thank-you.

Body

Now, using the power of your imagination and visualization, imagine that this bubble around your heart is expanding to encompass your entire body. Your body sits comfortably encased in this clear, quiet, energized bubble. What do you notice about your body at this time? Do you notice any particular energy or frequency? Is there anything special about the feeling or vibration? Engage with this energy as much as possible and ask your body, "Is there anything I need to know at this time?"

What, if anything, do you perceive? If you do receive something, acknowledge the information with a thank-you.

Room

Next, imagine that this bubble around your body is expanding to encompass the entire room. The room, along with everyone and everything in it, is comfortably encased in this energized cocoon. What do you notice about the room? Do you become aware of sounds that you didn't notice before? Are you aware of energies you weren't aware of before? Is there anything particularly attention-worthy about the room?

Using the power of your intention, move your awareness from place to place in the room. Shift your focus to the window or to a certain sound or to a certain piece of furniture. Notice what you notice about each different connection. When you have done that a few times, focus again on the entire room. Engage with this energy as much as possible and ask the room, "Is there anything I need to know at this time?"

What, if anything, do you perceive? If you do receive something, acknowledge the information with a thank-you.

City

Now imagine this bubble around the room is expanding to encompass the entire city you are in. Everyone and everything within the boundaries of the city is now comfortably encased in this protective bubble.

What do you immediately notice about the city? Do you become aware of a particular sound or feeling that the city is presenting to you? Is there anything attention-worthy about this sensation? Engage with this feeling as much as possible and ask the city, "Is there anything I need to know at this time?" What, if anything, do you perceive? If you notice anything, acknowledge it with a thank-you.

Earth

Next, expand your bubble to encompass the entire planet. Every living creature, every building, every river, every plant, stone, and tree is now comfortably encased in this energetic cocoon. What do you notice about the planet? Do you become aware of a particular sound or feeling that the planet is presenting to you? Is there anything special about this sensation?

Engage with it as much as possible, and ask the earth, "Is there anything I need to know at this time?" What, if anything, do you perceive? If you notice a response, acknowledge it with a thank-you.

Milky Way

Now, expand this bubble to encompass the entire solar system. Every planet, star, meteor, black hole, and bit of cosmic dust is now comfortably encased in this energetic cocoon. What do you notice about the solar system? Do you become aware of a particular sound or feeling that it is presenting to you? Is there anything special about this sensation?

Engage with it as much as possible and ask the solar system, "Is there anything I need to know at this time?" What, if anything, do you perceive? If you notice a response, acknowledge it with a thank-you.

Universe

Now expand this bubble to encompass the entire universe. Every field of energy, every atom, every life-form, every star and planet, past, present, and future, is now comfortably encased in this energetic cocoon. What do you notice about the universe? Do you become aware of a particular sound or feeling that the universe is presenting to you? Is there anything special about this sensation?

Engage with it as much as possible and ask the universe, "Is there anything I need to know at this time?" What, if anything, do you perceive? If you notice a response, acknowledge it with a thank-you.

Now simply spend a bit of time in this place of expanded awareness. What, if anything, have you noticed about your body? What, if anything, have you noticed about your mind? How does this place of awareness feel to you? Do your best to recognize and become intimate with this sensation.

Returning Home

When you feel you are ready to return, simply retrace your steps of awareness backward. Imagine that the cocoon of light is shrinking to the size of the solar system. Slowly it grows smaller still, and now it holds only the earth. It continues to get smaller and now holds only the city you are in. Then smaller still, until it holds only the room you are in. Then smaller, encompassing only your body. Then smaller, holding only your heart.

Stay here in this heart space for a few more moments. See if you can increase the amplitude of the feeling of peace and appreciation in your heart. Allow this feeling to once again saturate every part of your body, mind, and soul. From this place of awareness, once again ask your heart, "Is there anything I need to know at this time?" Notice what you notice, and if you perceive a response, acknowledge it with a thank-you.

Before you return to your usual activities, write down what you perceived as direct guidance or information in response to the questions you asked. See if it correlates to any situation, circumstance, or issue you may be working on in your life at this time. If it does, see how you can use it to heal, improve, or otherwise change that circumstance.

Welcome back. I hope you enjoyed your adventure.

PART III

THE FACETS OF
FIRST INTELLIGENCE

Learning the Language of Intuition

CHAPTER 7

THE TRINITY OF MIND

You cannot solve a problem from the same level of mind that created it.

— ALBERT EINSTEIN

As you may have noticed by now, intuition is not a function strictly limited to one body part, nor is it limited to one particular style or process of communication. It is a holistic function of the entire human structure: physically, spiritually, and mentally.

The *mind* processes that support and propel intuition are holistic, too. Remember that at the root of the unified field, which is the source of all creative information, is consciousness or mind. And in order to get our intuition to provide us with the information found in this field of information, we have to use *our* mind.

Mind is the middle ground between spirit and matter. But *how* do we use our mind to play this role, and *what* part of the mind are we using when we do so? It is not enough to simply say, "Use your mind," because the mind is a multidimensional, multilevel system of multitasking superpowers. We possess one mind, but there are multiple facets of it continuously at work. The information these facets perceive and feed to our other facets is determined by our level of consciousness, our focus, and the rate of energetic frequency we are supplying to it at any given moment.

BEING A BIOLOGICAL ANTENNA

In order to gather intuitive information, you do *not* have to project your thoughts anywhere. Nor does your intelligence have to go on a hunt through space and time for what it needs. We are directly and constantly linked to the information we seek, because we are the access point continuously connected to and communicating with the field.

The information we seek is constantly vibrating around us, and it is our job to align our mind processes so we can perceive that information. When we do that, the solution or idea we need appears in our awareness.

When our mind is calibrated for the intuitive information we are looking for, it vibrates at a specific frequency; we literally become a biological antenna. The information within the unified field that

Figure 10. Our biological antenna in the field

matches our intuitive request vibrates at that same frequency. And when the two frequencies metaphorically bump into each other, they form an interference pattern that shows up in the field as a *new* pattern or frequency. This new vibration is the energetic footprint, or source code, of the intuitive hit, the precognition, or the inner vision. As long as we are able to maintain our initial mind frequency, we can recognize this new interference pattern and use the information held within it to guide us to solutions we seek.

Because *we* are the source of the intuitive request, and we are inside the field at the same time, *we are* the meeting point of both waves. We are at the epicenter of the interference pattern. Which means all this transmitting, receiving, and perceiving is happening within our consciousness, is reflected on the inner screen of our mind, and is happening with no limitation imposed by space or time.

TUNING THE ANTENNA

In order to properly activate our biological antenna, we must amplify and direct certain facets of our mind function at specific times and quiet the rest. To a certain degree we already use this process every moment of the day, but we are completely unaware of it.

Mind is a *principle*, which means it operates by specific rules and laws. These laws are constant. They work in the same way, and produce the same results, regardless of whether you understand or believe in them.

True intuition is known to occur during an integrated communication between the three *facets* of mind — the superconscious mind, the conscious mind, and the subconscious mind — and the two *levels*: the higher mind and the lower mind.

The "Facets of Mind" table on the next page illustrates the multidimensional process of mind and how each facet operates within the intuitive process.

Facet of Mind	Location	Energetic Construct	Creative Skill	Level of Mind
Super-conscious	Soul	Spiritual	Inspiration/ desire	Higher
Conscious	Brain	Physical	Intention/ choice	Higher or lower
Subconscious	Heart	Emotional	Imagination/ creativity	Higher or lower

THE TRINITY

Just as there is a potent combination of intelligence in the body, so too is there a powerful team of mind functions that, when focused and used in alignment with each of their highest intuitive attributes, allows us access to truly evolutionary wisdom. Knowing how each of these attributes works and communicates with the others allows us to integrate all aspects of our energetic thought process and use it in a specific way to gain specific and successful results.

The Superconscious Mind

This mind is our infinite, higher-dimensional awareness that both holds and is the origin of all creation — the codes and energies for all things, ideas, and realities that have ever existed or will ever exist. It is completely spiritual in nature and has no material aspect. Its energetic source is viewed as the soul. Its creative superpowers are inspiration, planting desire, and causation. It speaks as intuition via the direct voice of the higher mind. It exists beyond space and time, and it governs the beginning and the end of the intuitive process.

The superconscious mind is the intelligence within us that creates and supports every function of our body. It knows precisely what to do to heal a cut, grow a hair, create a baby, or cure a disease. This is the all-knowing aspect of our intelligence that is able to identify what is true and what is false, enabling us to intuitively discern what is truly in our best interests and to direct ourselves to an evolutionary outcome. It sees higher possibilities and solutions that are not based in our previously learned knowledge or current experience.

The Conscious Mind

The second facet of mind is the conscious, or thinking, mind — the part of mind that controls our ideas, attitudes, and behaviors — and it has the power to deliberately select a destiny. It is material in nature and communicates through the language of the five senses. The brain is viewed as its energetic source. Its creative superpowers are intention and empowered choice. It directs its will through the voice of either the higher mind or the lower mind, depending on an individual's level of consciousness at the moment. It governs the second step in the intuitive process.

Conscious mind has the power to *choose* or *intend*, which makes it extremely powerful. The power of *conscious* choice stabilizes the process of creation, which means that life is continuously happening, and that new ideas, new relationships, new feelings, and new possibilities are constantly snapping in and out of possibility in every moment.

Choice, as a function of mindful will and focus, isolates a single specific possibility out of that wide field of all possibility and begins to stabilize it. Empowered choice begins the process of isolating a frequency of potential and "cuts it from the herd," so to speak, to begin the process of bringing it into being.

For most people, the conscious mind is in control only about 5 percent of the time. Because of this unconsciousness, the energy of choice does not have a persistent effect on the energetic field of information. This is why, once you consciously stop intending something, the effect on the field is not maintained. So your ideas, dreams, or desires do not go anywhere or become anything. However, with the development of an expanded understanding and awareness, the conscious mind does have the power to engage with and influence the subconscious mind, to ultimately implant the seed of choice or desire in order to bring it to fruition.

The Subconscious Mind

The creative mind, the third facet of mind involved in the intuitive process, is the part of you that holds every single memory of your lifetime. It is linked to the memories of every other person through the collective consciousness. It is emotional by nature, and the heart is viewed as its energetic source. Its superpowers are innovation and creativity. It operates compulsively — that is, with no will of its own — via the voice of the higher or the lower mind, depending on the level of consciousness that has influenced it over time. It is the third step in the intuitive process.

The subconscious mind is a massive storage unit of information, and it represents 95 percent of our programming. When we live life "unconsciously," *this* is the mind in charge of our attitudes, actions, and behaviors. Its actions are automatic and based in past experience. It cannot discern what is good or bad, positive or negative, life affirming or life negating. While it has memory, it doesn't have the ability to consciously claim, "I choose to heal; I choose to be wealthy; I choose to be loved and to be loving." It simply does not possess that level of power.

However, the subconscious mind does possess the power to come up with decidedly unique and innovative ways to fashion and compulsively generate outcomes or produce realities based on the information that has been entered into it over its lifetime. If it has been fed with life-affirming information, the results will reflect those affirmations. If it has been fed with depleted or diminishing information, the results will reflect that information instead. The subconscious mind does what the conscious mind tells it to do, and it will do it with or without our awareness.

THE CYCLE OF THE INTUITIVE MIND

The process of intuition unfolds as follows:

1. Inspiration strikes. The superconscious mind presents us with a dream, desire, or hope for a specific direction or certain outcome.
2. In order for the nonphysical desire to become a reality in the material realm, it needs a physical construct to bring it into being. Symbolically speaking, the desire "drops" from higher energy to lower energy so it can move from spirit (potential) into matter (reality).
3. The desire is acknowledged by the conscious mind, which makes a choice to follow that desire (or not) and to do whatever it takes to create the outcome (or not).

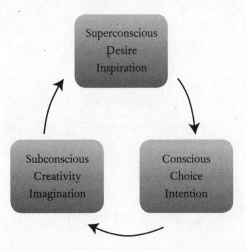

Figure 11. The cycle of the intuitive mind

4. Using the elevated, coherent patterns of peace to open and soften the subconscious mind, the conscious mind directs its thoughts and intentions so the seeds can take root.

5. The conscious and subconscious minds then surrender the desire to the power of the superconscious mind, knowing that the ultimate creative power of this level of mind will bring it into being.

6. When an energetic saturation occurs and these seeds become solidified within both the conscious mind and the subconscious mind, a shift occurs in the field, which triggers the superconscious mind to change the expression of all the energetic codes of the mind, and a new reality presents itself.

THE HIGHER AND LOWER MINDS

In addition to the three facets of mind, there are two levels of mind in operation at any given moment. When we engage in the intuitive process through the energetic structure of the lower mind, we gain only information that leads us to make the same limiting choices as in the past, which leads us to the same limited outcomes. If we want access to the powerful information stored in the kingdom of heaven, for example, we cannot expect to find it hidden in the basement.

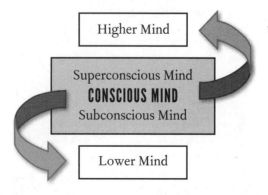

Figure 12. The choice point of the conscious mind

This decision to access the field through the higher mind or the lower mind is once again a choice point that is directed and decided upon by the conscious mind.

Higher Mind

Our higher mind is the physical representative of our nonphysical soul, and it speaks to us through the voice of our intuition as the link to the superconscious mind of the creative field. Although it is physical, it is able to transcend the boundaries of matter, time, and space and to operate beyond ego; it is associated with all the noble truths linked to the principles of life. This is the aspect of self that guides us to safety and ensures that we are greater than our perceived physical limitations; that anything is possible; that we are continually guided, protected; and that we are endlessly loved.

This level of mind has a low density and a high frequency and is more spirit than matter. It is *causative* and is the source of ground-breaking ideas, innovative solutions, paradigm-changing outcomes, and new realities. It is the true source of our creative power.

Considerations: See if you can recall moments in your life when your higher mind was in charge. There may not be a lot of them, but everyone has had at least one moment when things were easy, fun, and filled with joy.

- It may have been a moment that brought you to tears, or that opened your heart to awe and wonder, or that made the hair on your arms stand up in a good way.
- It may have been at the birth of a child, or a powerful moment in nature, or a moment in the company of a fabulous group of loving friends, or a moment of deep introspection.
- It may even have occurred in a moment of deep pain and despair.

Such a moment reveals itself when we are so present in the current moment that all the incoherence caused by the lower mind fades away and we perceive, with all our intelligence systems, the beauty and perfection around us. It snaps us to attention, if only for a brief moment and says to us, "See this beauty, feel this power? *This* is who you really are!" This is the true voice of our intuition.

Lower Mind

The lower mind is the physical representation of our wounded or damaged ego and speaks to us through the distorted belief that we are separate from the creative power of universal intelligence. Our lower mind is also known as the deceiver, and it likes to convince us that we are limited in every way — including time, space, and resources — and that the only way to succeed in life is by manipulating the physical world in any way possible.

Its guidance is heavily steeped in negative emotion. It leads us to take actions that may not be in our best interests, and which enmesh us in old patterns of attitude and action that keep us spinning on the wheel of karmic repetition.

Characterized by high density and low frequency, the lower mind is more matter than spirit. This level of mind exists as a conditional effect of situations, experiences, or realities around it. It has no ability whatsoever to generate causative energy that can alter or heal a situation. It has no creative power.

Unfortunately the lower mind is the one that most people continually use. It certainly is the one running most governments and ruling political choices these days, and it is definitely the one in charge of the financial, medical, educational, and religious establishments globally.

Considerations: Take a moment or two and reflect on the times when you have been stuck in your lower mind.

- It may have been during an argument with a coworker or spouse, or while you felt trapped in line at the bank.
- It may have been when you got cut off by someone in traffic,

or when you were worried about paying your bills, trying to find a solution at work, or dealing with difficult relatives.

- It may have been, as it is with so many people, whenever you looked in the mirror.

The lower mind is an equal-opportunity frustrater. It likes to believe that it knows all the answers and has all the solutions, but it does not and never will have the power of wisdom or true intelligence. The table bellow lists the attributes and energies of the higher and lower minds. Becoming intimate with their differences will empower you to distinguish between the two and gain greater precision with your intuitive awareness.

Higher Mind	Lower Mind
Life affirming	Life negating
Optimistic	Pessimistic
Generous	Selfish
Enthusiastic	Indifferent
Based in abundance	Based in lack
Balanced	Unbalanced
Successful	Limited
Compassionate	Cruel
Causative	Noncausative
Innovative	Regimented
Win-Win	Win-Lose
Timeless	Restricted
Responsive	Reactive
Coherent	Distorted
Integrated	Compartmentalized
Allowing	Controlling
Peaceful	Fearful
Exists in present moment	Exists in past and future

Hanging out in the lower mind is a habit you will have to break. The most powerful way to usurp this dictator of dismay is to learn to recognize when you are stuck in its influential field and to make a *conscious* choice to move into the higher realms of mind by focusing on and generating the energy of peace. In fact, using the power of your *will* is the only way out from under the power of the lower mind. The easiest way to break that control is by focusing on the foundation of peace, precision, and perception. At first this will require deliberate and continual focus, but eventually the practice of being in the higher mind will become automatic and organic, just like riding a bike or driving a car. Remind yourself that if you have learned to do either of those things, you have already mastered this mind process, and that what you did then, you can do again. So, for the purpose of moving forward in your intuitive practice with a sense of ease and certainty, *choose* to consider yourself already successful.

PLAYING THE MIND GAME

Think of the relationship between your superconscious, conscious, and subconscious minds as a game of cosmic baseball played out on the field of dreams that represents all possibility. Except, in this game, every player on the field is you: your superconscious mind is the pitcher, your conscious mind is the player at bat, and your subconscious mind is every other player on the field.

The superconscious mind winds up and pitches the conscious mind a great desire, one that has come from the field of all possibility and is crafted especially for you. It throws this pitch in a perfect arc right in front of you, across home plate.

Your conscious mind sees it and really wishes it had the courage to take a swing at it. But there is some lame guy in the stands who heckles the conscious mind. This brute in the bleachers is the lower mind, and it shouts at you to ignore the desire that has been tossed your way, because you are too old, or because you don't have enough experience, or because if you swing at it you are going to miss and look like a real idiot to everyone watching.

So you stand there at home base and let that heckler tell you what to do, and you consciously decide to let that desire fly right past you. You don't move from where you started, and life stays the same. But that's just fine and dandy, because the superconscious mind has endless patience and an endless source of supply. Since it has no relation to time, it will patiently and continuously toss desires your way. And so it throws another perfect pitch right into the sweet spot across home plate.

You let the desire whiz past you once more, and you don't move. You are well aware that you are ignoring these desires because of what that lousy heckler is telling you from the bleachers. And it is starting to really frustrate you, not only because part of you knows what he's saying is untrue, but also because you've been standing still for so long, hovering over home plate while your dreams for a greater future are whizzing by, that it's causing your body to ache and seize up. For a while, you could stand still and ignore these pitches, but now the pain has built up, and you can no longer ignore it.

Once again, you are thrown the perfect desire, but this time your conscious mind ignores the yammering of the lower mind and swings. The bat and the ball, the mind and the desire, make contact, and the desire soars out over the field.

In that moment the dream becomes alive, and possibility becomes activated. A powerful shift occurs and now all the players on the field are aligned with a common goal, even and especially those who once stood in opposition. Now all levels of mind are moving: the cheerleaders of the higher mind line the outfield and wildly urge you on as you run from base to base, while the players of the subconscious mind throw the ball from one player to another, coordinating with one another to work out the creative details to help drive the conscious mind home.

These creative details appear to the conscious mind as intuitive ideas, innovative strategies, coincidences, and synchronicities; and the conscious mind pays attention, acknowledges these things, and takes action to move ahead.

Once in a while the conscious mind may stumble or fall between bases, and occasionally it may need a brief time-out so that the timing of different moving parts can be coordinated, or so that it can rest. But when the conscious mind consistently chooses to act, this propels the desire to fruition. The only way this can fail is if the conscious player chooses to walk off the field.

The conscious mind finds itself so deeply engaged in this new effort that it no longer hears the noise from the bleachers, especially not the disturbed mutterings from the lower mind. Those chants that once so depleted its power no longer hold any sway. But no matter where the conscious mind is on the field, it always has a direct view of the superconscious mind, which stands on the elevated pitcher's mound watching, supporting, and guiding the conscious mind the entire way.

With this increased momentum, the conscious mind's ability to use the power of its spiritual desire to propel itself to a greater destiny becomes clear. Home base is visible. There can be no stopping now, and the conscious mind, still committed to its victory and supported by the other players, makes its final charge home to complete its assignment. With the power and courage stimulated by the journey, the player slides heartfirst into home base. The desire has been answered. A piece of destiny has been achieved.

The players take a brief moment to celebrate this success, but because all things are in a constant state of growth, and because new dreams for the future are always coming our way, the superconscious once again reaches into the field of all possibility. It grabs another desire, winds up to make another perfect pitch, and the game continues.

POSTGAME SHOW

So, as you can see, there is a perfect balance and symmetry to the processes that our mind uses to achieve a beneficial outcome. You can also see that every single aspect and function of our humanity can be used to its highest level of proficiency. Nothing is overlooked, nothing is wasted — everything we are gifted with on a physical and spiritual level has perfect purpose.

Now that you know all the players in this intuitive-mind game, it is time to combine all this biological information and energetic insight and put them to work.

CHAPTER 8

THE FOUR LEVELS
OF INTUITION

Knowing others is intelligence; knowing yourself is true wisdom.
Mastering others is strength; mastering yourself is true power.
If you realize that, you have enough, you are truly rich.

— LAO-TZU, TAO TE CHING

Part of the precision involved in developing our First Intelligence concerns becoming intimately aware of the different levels, styles, and identifying markers our intuition uses to communicate, and of how each level uses its own special attributes to serve us in specific situations and to suit certain needs. Many of the misinterpretations of and superstitions about intuition are perpetuated by people who aren't fluent in the language. Common yet deeply toxic misconceptions about what intuition is and how it is developed stand as some of the most limiting obstacles we might face, and they create false ideas that block, if not completely obliterate, our ability to use it in any meaningful way.

It is crucial to understand what intuition *is* and what it *isn't*, so that as you progress through your practice and study you develop an intimacy with how your higher wisdom is communicated to you. Just as we have multiple levels of perception, we also have multiple levels of intuitive communication. Intuition operates in our body and nervous system on levels that range from basic, binary, survival-based communications to complete conversations that are elegant, sophisticated, and evolved.

LEVEL 1: GUT INSTINCT

Attributes: safety, security, and survival.

We have all heard of this level of intuition, and most of us can recall a time when we have recognized it or felt its presence in our lives. And depending on our level of trust, we may have followed the instinct. Gut instinct may be the best-known and most mainstream interpretation of intuition, but it is only a small part of the entire intelligence system. We should not depend on it alone to guide us to our highest potential or outcome.

Instinct is a survival mechanism present in every living life-form. *Merriam-Webster's* defines it as the inherited and unalterable tendency of an organism to make a complex and specific response to environmental stimuli without involving reason. Human beings use it, monkeys use it, plants use it, and amoebas use it; it is the base function of all living systems, and it serves the drive to survive.

At its most basic, or material, level, an organism is capable of only two modes of operation: growth or survival. If a body receives the impression from its environment that it is safe, that body will automatically take life-affirming, life-expanding, *growth*-based actions that allow all systems to function at peak levels. When the environment is perceived as unsafe, that same organism will shift into *survival* mode, and all those life-affirming actions will stop, so that the energy can be used by the organism to simply stay alive.

The intelligence housed in the gut is not sophisticated enough to provide us with higher wisdom. It is simple, basic, and binary, which means it communicates through the *feeling* of opposites and uses impressions such as yes or no, stop or go, safe or unsafe to convey its message.

Figure 13. The first level of intuition: gut instinct

High-powered business executives and law enforcement officers tend to rely on this level of intuition, because in their world many situations *are* often perceived as life or death. That situation may be a business transaction that will determine the outcome of a major deal, which may mean the survival or destruction of a company. In the case of law enforcement, an officer entering the home of a suspect may literally face a life-or-death situation.

In the moments when gut instinct is communicating the message "Unsafe," you may feel nauseated or get a feeling of indigestion. You may notice a shift in energy or a change in temperature, or you may suddenly feel depressed, anxious, or worried. This is the primary level of your First Intelligence saying, "No, thank you. This is not safe. This will cost us energy in some way. This is not appropriate for us." Do *not* ignore these impressions.

On the other hand, because life-affirming energies, too, exist in our environment, gut instinct provides guidance when it recognizes influences that support growth or expansion or that align with our highest good in some other way.

As a part of becoming fluent in the language of First Intelligence, you must learn to recognize the difference between the two polarities (growth and survival) and how they are uniquely presented within your body. When a growth opportunity presents itself, the wisdom of the body says, "We are safe here. Yes, please. More, please. This feels good."

When your gut instinct is operating, it will answer such questions as: "Is this choice/person/relationship in my best interests? Can I thrive in this environment? Will this meet my deepest needs?"

JENNA

I was ready to buy my first home and scheduled an afternoon to look at four or five different properties with my real estate agent. When we walked into the first house, which was a brand-new listing and wasn't even on my list for that day, I took two or three steps into the foyer and felt my entire body open up and feel lighter. There was a feeling of butterflies in my stomach as I walked into the living room with a sense of "I belong here."

I said to my agent, "Uh-oh," because I knew in that moment that this house would be my home. We looked through the rest of the residence, and the feeling of safety and comfort continued to grow stronger.

Keeping an open mind and knowing my agent had made arrangements for us to look at other properties, I agreed to go look at the other houses on our list. As we crossed the threshold of the next house, my stomach dropped, I felt nauseated, and my palms started to sweat. My agent had already made her way into one of the first bedrooms, so I followed her, only to have the awful feeling intensify. I didn't need to see anything else; I

looked at her and said, "Nope," and walked back out the way
we came. It just didn't feel right. When we got to the driveway, I
said to her, "I know I should look at as many houses as possible
before making a decision, but my gut just knows that the first
house is my house. I have to trust that."

Thirty days later, the first house was my house; and I
learned afterward that a woman had been murdered in the sec-
ond house. My gut instinct served me well.

Considerations

- When have you noticed your gut instinct at work? Do
  you tend to notice it more in *survival* situations or *growth*
  situations?
- What were the circumstances involved? Who were the people involved? What was at stake for you? (A job, a relationship, money, status, reputation?)
- Please identify how gut instinct *feels* to you. Where do you
  notice it the most in your body? (Just because it is called *gut*
  instinct does not mean the gut is the only place you will feel
  it. Please notice all impressions.)
- How does your gut instinct communicate with you in a *sur-*
  vival situation?
- How does it communicate with you in a *growth* situation?
- Think of a specific time when you felt your gut instinct. Did
  you pay attention to the impression? Did you respond to the
  impressions? If you did, why did you? If you didn't, why
  didn't you? Often people (especially women) will say that
  they don't follow their instinct because they don't want to
  be rude or appear to be bitchy. Your ability to identify your
  blind spots — the habitual patterns you follow that keep
  you from trusting your First Intelligence — will make your

instincts more precise and teach you to trust yourself when your gut instinct kicks in.

• What was the outcome of the situation? Did it ultimately place you in survival or growth mode?

Practice

Make a commitment this week to notice when your gut — and the rest of your body — is communicating with you. Based on what you discovered in the preceding list of considerations, pay attention to how you feel when interacting with other people or when making decisions about which actions to take. Notice whether your body shifts into growth or survival mode. Commit to following the feelings of those impressions without judging them or explaining them to anyone. Allow yourself to have fun with this experiment and see if you can begin to develop an intimacy with this first facet of your intuitive intelligence.

LEVEL 2: HEART-BASED INTELLIGENCE

Attributes: courage, compassion, and communication.

As we move upward in the physical body, the level of subtle energy found within the Trilateral Intelligence System rises, too.

The heart is the esoteric middleman, the passageway between heaven and earth, spirit and matter. And it is the chamber through which the energetic frequencies of the universe are translated, ultimately determining how we interact with and communicate with everything on our material plane. The intelligence of the heart encourages us to learn to live in both worlds, so that we can use the wisdom of our higher mind to guide us as we navigate through this adventure we call life.

The heart encourages us to adopt the higher vibratory practices of courage, compassion, and care and use them to communicate and connect with all other life-forms in our environment. It encourages us to communicate with the environment itself. The heart values both aspects of our being, the material and the spiritual, and honors them equally, knowing full well that the only way we will achieve our highest potential and our soul's destiny is *through* the vehicle of the physical world. Nothing is diminished.

Often the wisdom of the heart comes into direct conflict with the expectations or material concerns of the lower mind or wounded ego. For example, the wisdom of the heart may tell us it is time to move on from a relationship that is preventing us from growing, but our fearful lower mind will deny this wisdom because it fears being alone, or never finding love again, or not being able to make ends meet.

This level of intuition also lets us feel compassion and empathy for others. It guides us to what is appropriate to say or do in moments of need and allows us to connect and communicate in often unspoken ways and to bond with people, animals, and places in ways that cannot be described by words or rational thought.

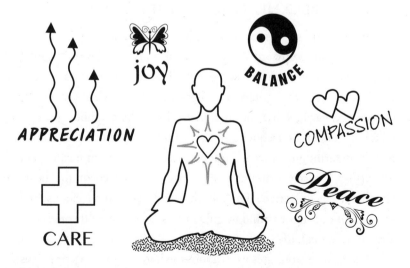

Figure 14. The second level of intuition: heart-based intelligence

Heart-based intelligence also provides direction that helps us find what might benefit us creatively, spiritually, and communally. It tends to recognize the energies of inspiration, creativity, and connection — or the lack of it — and signals the need for growth as a "knowing" in the heart.

This center of wisdom, when balanced in the foundational energy of peace or coherence, prompts us to ask the questions such as: "Is my life filled with beauty? Do I love what I do? How can I discover my joy? What would I do if I were not afraid? Am I bringing the best of myself to my life and the world?"

DEIDRE

I had been working at the same place for many years, and I liked it and the people there, but something inside me knew it was time to move on. I didn't have another job lined up or know what I wanted to do next, but I knew in my heart that it was time to go. I didn't dislike where I was, but it didn't nourish me in the way that it had at the beginning, when I was just starting my career.

Initially I felt guilty about leaving, which in the past would have kept me from actually moving on, and I could feel the fear initiated by my "thinking mind" about how I would make ends meet if I were to leave. But when I stayed committed to cultivating a peaceful and coherent focus, and could silence the chatter of that fearful thinking, my heart let me know that it was all right; I had done and learned what I needed to and it was time to move on.

With that guidance I gave my boss thirty days' notice. I was able to speak directly from my heart and let him know how much I had enjoyed working there and how I appreciated what they had done for me. With a referral in hand, I made it my priority, in following the wisdom of my heart, to find a position that inspired me, filled me with energy, and was aligned with the things that have meaning for me. Within two weeks I found a new position, with about the same pay, working in a creative field that I really enjoy. In the past I would have second-guessed myself, worried, or felt guilty about leaving. For now, I will trust what I feel in my heart and not fear it.

Considerations

- When have you noticed the wisdom of your heart at work in your life? Does it make itself known in personal or intimate situations? Do you notice it in work or professional dynamics?

- How does it make itself known to you? Does it tend to happen spontaneously, or do you have to access it in an intentional way? What were the circumstances involved? Who were the people involved? What was at stake for you? (A job, a relationship, money, status, reputation?)

- Were you able to follow the direction immediately? Were you frightened about taking action? Did you avoid listening to it? Did you take action?

- If you did take action, what were the results? If you didn't, why not and what have the results been? Are you able to recognize the times when your heart guides you in a certain direction and you ignore it or talk yourself out of it? How do you justify that rejection of information?

- How has your heart's intelligence helped you communicate with others? Are you able to identify the situations that shut your heart down? Why do you think that happens? How do those situations turn out? What, if anything, can you learn from those situations now, and how would you change them in the future?

- Is there something in your past that your heart has directed you to do that you could still take action on? Are you willing to take that action now? What is that action?

Practice

Throughout the week, take notice of how your heart feels in certain situations. When you meet with or converse with someone, engage him with your heart. Listen and speak from this center of empathetic power. Notice if your heart is guiding you in one way or another about what to say or do. If you have an important question you need guidance on, turn it over to the power of your heart and listen carefully to what it tells you.

LEVEL 3: VISIONARY POWER

Attributes: imagination, visionary certainty, and creative possibility.

The third level of intuitive intelligence is found in the mystical and often misunderstood power of extrasensory perception (ESP). This seat of intelligence is thought to be located in the pineal gland, the pituitary gland, and the supporting structures of the hypothalamus. But more and more scientific findings have revealed that the brain itself is holographic, meaning that each cell of the brain contains the potential of the whole brain. In other words, it is possible for every part of the brain to have telepathic and intuitive power.

When these structures are stimulated by strong magnetic fields provided either by external sources or by the power of the heart itself, they release certain neurotransmitters, including DMT (dimethyltryptamine), which induces the phenomena of expanded spiritual vision, lucid dreaming, and other elevated psychic events. When this region of a person's brain is naturally empowered, or it develops through meditative practices, she is able to perceive and engage with nonlocal and nonphysical information in a directed manner and use it in a way determined by choice instead of happenstance.

This is the level of intuition at which extraordinary solutions, alternate ways of doing things, and groundbreaking new ideas are commonplace. These solutions would have never been considered by your rational intellect, yet they hold the key to elegant results.

Figure 15. The third level of intuition: visionary power

Because this level of seeing allows a person to experience and perceive information from other realms, both higher *and* lower, it is crucial to complete as much spiritual work and development as possible. This way you can be certain that, in all moments, your vibrations, intentions, and attitudes always align with only the highest good and the most beneficial outcome for all.

When this center of wisdom is active and balanced in the foundation of peace or coherence, it guides us to ask questions such as: "What do I see as a solution or possibility? Is there something I am overlooking? What dreams do I have for my future that I haven't given myself permission to make into reality?"

EMMIE

My poor dog, Gizmo, was suffering terribly from skin allergies. Summer is always a rough time for her because the heat and the insects really irritate her sensitive skin. I was deeply concerned about what I could do to alleviate her pain and heal the lesions she had developed.

One morning while I was brushing my teeth, Gizmo came into the bathroom and sat at my feet and started to scratch aggressively. It broke my heart to see her so uncomfortable. I stood at the sink, closed my eyes, generated peace and coherence, and asked the question "What can I do to ease Gizmo's pain?" Instantly the word calendula *flashed in my mind. I had never heard this word before.*

"What?" I asked aloud.

"Ca-len-du-la," was the reply once more.

I went and looked up the term calendula *online, and it turned out to be a natural, floral remedy that, when applied to the skin, reduces pain and swelling and speeds the healing of chronic sores and wounds. And it was available at my local health food store. I laughed to myself, amused by the potency and directness of the answer.*

I picked up a tube of calendula ointment and applied it to Gizmo's skin irritations. Within days they had all begun to heal, and within a week her skin was perfectly clear. We never used another conventional skin treatment again, and now, if either of us ever has a bug bite or skin irritation, calendula is the only thing we use to heal it.

Considerations

- How has sixth-sense intelligence appeared in your life before? What sense does it tend to use most prominently?

Sight, smell, sound, taste, or touch? When you experienced it, how did it *feel* in your body? (Please be specific here.)

- What were you doing when you had the experience? How often do you remember having noticed it?
- Did you follow the guidance? Why or why not? What were the results of your choice? Does the guidance tend to be about random, everyday things, or does it appear when things are crucial or life altering?
- Have you ever told other people about your experiences? If so, what was their feedback? Supportive? Interested? They thought you were nuts?
- Would you be comfortable with having access to this intelligence all the time? Would you be able to trust it? What validation from the expanded sensory experiences would you need in order to allow them to consistently guide you?

Practice

Throughout the week, take notice of how you are receiving inner vision or inner sensory perceptions. Pay attention to ideas, images, or other sensory impulses that seem to pop into your head from out of nowhere. See if these impressions provide you with a solution or idea that can serve you or in some way guide you to a potentially positive outcome. If you have an important question you need guidance on, turn it over to your visionary power and see if anything "pops up."

LEVEL 4: THE CONNECTION TO UNIVERSAL WISDOM

Attributes: universal awareness and unity consciousness.

The fourth level of intuitive intelligence is the most nonphysical of the group. It is said to be based, physically, at the top of the head and, energetically, just above it. This is the doorway between our physical being and the invisible realm of the unified field and all universal wisdom.

This intelligence, too, uses our expanded senses of sight, touch, and so on, but it uses them only because, while we are still alive, we process information received from the environment. This intelligence is often activated during deep meditation or advanced awareness practices, and it is sometimes reported after near-death experiences or times of great stress or trauma, such as a car accident, surgery, and incidents of abuse.

This is the wisdom we may receive when *all* aspects of the human mind are turned down or turned off, that exists beyond all ideas or perceptions of the physical body, time, or space. This cosmic perspective puts us in touch with the timeless essence that is our soul, and it places all things in our lives, both those perceived as good and those perceived as bad, in relation to the entire universal picture. It removes our perceptions that create obstacles to connecting with universal wisdom and gives us an opportunity to experience and identify with the energetic field of intelligence that operates entirely on the foundation of peace and well-being.

Whenever I speak of this level of intelligence, I am reminded of reports of the stories that astronauts brought back with them from space. Many of them reported that once they left the earth's gravitational field, they transcended the energetic mind-soup that is the human race and experienced a moment that was hard to describe. They said they felt a connection to all the stars and planets, to all the people, plants, and animals, and that they recognized a profound relationship to the field of information and intelligence that had created them.

The highest level of intuition that humans can reach while in human form is the one that allows us, as finite, physical beings, to access the realm of all things and to become consciously aware of our connection *to* and ability to create *with* the intelligence that is the source of our reality. For a time, we become limitless and we identify with the truth of our highest spiritual dimension.

Figure 16. The fourth level of intuition: connection to universal intelligence

When we are aligned with this level of intelligence, we recognize that all things in life are valuable and appropriate. And we trust that all our needs will be met, that we are safe regardless of external circumstances, and that we have the power within us to change and heal our lives if we so choose. We begin to appreciate all aspects of our material form and realize that they are part of the story of our evolution.

Here there are no questions. There is only consciousness.

GINA

I hit the curve doing seventy. Obviously I was driving too fast and not paying attention to the road. One second I was drinking a soda, tapping the wheel while listening to the radio, and the

next second my body was slamming over and over again into the roof of the car as it did a series of flips down the embankment. The interesting thing was that I watched it all from outside my body as it happened, sort of like watching a movie in the theater. I didn't feel any pain. I didn't notice any discomfort. I just watched and thought, "Isn't this interesting? I'm here, but not here. I'm in it, but not in it."

The tumble down the hill had to have lasted about fifteen seconds. You can fall a long way when speed and gravity kick in. The impact of the car against a tree at the bottom of the hill stopped me in a split second and ripped the vehicle in half. But I wasn't aware of time at all.

Once my mind was free of my body, there wasn't any time. There wasn't any pain. There wasn't any emotion. Just peace. Big, juicy, buzzy, vibrating peace. It was as if my soul did me a favor by pulling me out of my body while all this was happening so I wouldn't be distracted by the pain. As if someone or something wanted to say, "Hey, watch this now. Pay close attention. I don't want you to be freaked out by how uncomfortable it will be if you're still connected to your mind, so I'm gonna cut the connection for a moment and you can watch from here. You are safe always, even when your world is being turned upside down and split in two. None of this is you. None of this is yours. Remember this feeling, this peace thing. Remember it."

That was it. I woke up in the hospital after a few days in a coma, with a bunch of broken bones, a punctured lung, and a pretty big gash in my leg. But given the severity of the accident, I was pretty darn lucky. The memory of the crash felt more like a dream to me than reality, and I didn't have any of the typical feelings of trauma. What stood out as truly real was the memory of the message that none of my life was really mine, that peace

*was important above all things, and that I was supposed to hold
on to it.*

*That experience shaped how I navigated my healing pro-
cess and how I returned to living my life. I am different than
I was before. Less afraid, more calm, more confident. Now
whenever I come up against things in life, I realize that these
experiences really aren't who I am, that I am something larger,
more amazing, that simply holds these experiences but doesn't
become them. And I remember that peace and practice it as often
as possible.*

*That roll down the hill did turn my life upside down. In
that moment, I lost every idea about who I thought I was, and
I discovered the reality of who I am. I still have some scars, but
even those aren't who I am. I am that buzzy peace. That is the
source of me, and that is where all my wisdom and power lie.*

Considerations

- Have you ever experienced a moment of timelessness, when
  you were involved in something so deeply that time stopped
  or you lost track of yourself or of what you were doing?
  What were you doing in that moment? Can you identify
  the *feeling* associated with that experience? Describe it. Can
  you re-create that feeling in your body?
- Take a few moments right now to generate the same feeling you identified. Give yourself some time to "embody"
  it in every cell of your being. What do you notice in your
  body? What, if any, energy do you feel? Do you notice an
  expansion or contraction? Do you notice anything shifting
  or vibrating in your body?
- Where does your mind go when you are in this experience?
  What do you find yourself focusing on? Or is your mind
  still? Become intimate with this feeling. Notice everything

that accompanies it. Say quietly to yourself, "Yes, I will remember this."

- What, if anything, do you notice about how you feel about any of the current concerns or worries in your life? Is there some wisdom in that place of timelessness that you could apply to those situations?
- What is the message carried in that wisdom? Are you brave enough to follow it? Why or why not?

Practice

Throughout the week, pay attention to the tiny, fleeting moments when it feels as if you have lost track of time or when your awareness seems to be someplace beyond the physical limitations of your body. This may occur during your meditative practice, while you are exercising or being creative, or while you are simply going about your daily routine. These moments are usually brief, so when you notice one, acknowledge it and ask a question you would like some direction on. Then, with faith and certainty, turn this question over to this higher aspect of yourself that has understanding far beyond your limited perception, and expect to be given the answer in one way or another.

WHAT INTUITION IS AND WHAT IT ISN'T

Following are several understandings about what intuition *is* and *isn't*. These distinctions will assist you in further demystifying the process and will enable you to discern the subtle yet powerful differences between the tone and style of true intuitive perception and those of past emotional programming, learned behavior, and misguided understandings of the intuitive process. These clarifications will allow you to amplify and fine-tune your precision so that your accuracy and outcomes will become more and more reliable.

Intuition Is *Not* Based in Emotion

Intuition communicates in a *neutral, unemotional* fashion. The most common misconception about intuition, and why it tends to get a bad rap, especially in environments dominated by logical, rational, and, dare I say, masculine thinking, is the greatly erroneous contention that intuition is not to be trusted because it is based in emotion.

Since intuition is emotional*ly neutral*, there is no "charge" of opposites (right/wrong, fear/love, good/bad). This is because it stems from the highest level of mind, which is unchangeable, immovable, indestructible, and *beyond* emotion. The emotion tends to come the moment *after* you receive the information, or the "hit." As quick as thought, you *become* emotional because the information you perceive triggers fear, worry, or anxiety, because it requires you to *do* something that you may not feel comfortable doing. Or, conversely, it triggers emotions of ease, anticipation, or joy, because the direction is in alignment with your highest good. The emotion comes from your *response* to the intuitive wisdom, not from the wisdom itself.

Intuition Is Inner *Knowing*; It Is *Not* External Learning

"How do you know what you know when you know it?" This was the question I asked a room full of detectives in the first moments of a two-day workshop designed to amplify intuitive intelligence in police officers. I wanted to get a feel for the room and to see what they thought was going on when they got a hunch or an intuitive certainty about something.

Every one of the detectives admitted to having many intuitive experiences on and off the job. Some of them were willing to say they didn't really know what was involved in the process, but the majority of them said they believed their intuitive experiences were a result of their massive amount of training and their large number of years spent in law enforcement.

It is true that while on the job the officers take action based on impressions they perceive in the brain and body. But these "knowings" should be attributed to the automatic function of a brain that has studied, practiced, and experienced something so many times that the knowledge has been moved from the conscious part of the brain to the subconscious, or unconscious, part so the organ can conserve its energy to continue to store more information.

It is the brain on autopilot, where operations take place without conscious intervention. These unconscious states, while beneath awareness, are still experienced by our body as feelings, emotions, and mental impressions, and they significantly affect routine actions such as brushing our teeth and driving to work.

Modern computers and other forms of technology are designed to operate more intuitively — that is, to operate with greater creative ease and higher performance. But like the police detectives, these pieces of equipment are deeply coded and programmed so that their performance *seems* to appear intuitive. The "mind" of the computer has been taught what to do, and so it does everything it is supposed to do with seemingly magical skill. This ability, while interesting or inspiring, is *not* intuition. True intuitive intelligence is an inner *knowing*, a direct perception of and processing of information within the inner dimensions of mind, without access to previous study, knowledge, or experience. *It is knowing without having to go through the process of learning.*

Intuition Is Life Affirming

Intuition supports life at its highest levels of evolution and well-being and guides us so we can grow and thrive despite obstacles, regardless of how severe they may appear to our limited perceptions. This truth is reflected in the power of water to break down a mountain, a single acorn to produce an entire forest after a wildfire, or a tiny weed to crack a slab of concrete wide open so it can reach for greater light and potential.

Intuitive intelligence is highly energy efficient, and it guides us to our destiny via the path of least resistance, right action, and highest good. It guides us to solutions that are elegant and natural, that unfold without force, and that are advantageous to everyone involved. Intuitive intelligence understands that life supports life, and that to benefit one is to benefit the whole.

Intuition operates strictly in the present moment. It does not respond to past resentments or worries about the future. Its creative power lies in the eternal moment of "now," and it uses that point of stillness to propel itself forward, toward greater evolution.

You will know you are not connected to the wisdom of your intuition if

- you are upset about the past or worried about the future;
- you hear the words *can't, won't, shouldn't, don't,* or *what if;*
- you find yourself needing to control the details or outcome of a situation; or
- you find yourself being critical of yourself, those around you, or the situation you are in.

These descriptions of what intuition is or is not illustrate the positive markers of intuition at its best. As you further develop your intuitive practice, I encourage you to continually check in with yourself to see if the information you are receiving aligns with these principles. If it does not, then you may have more work to do to ensure that your energetic foundation is what it needs to be, so that you can properly engage with the field. If the information you receive is aligned, then you can go ahead and take the appropriate action to move toward your goal.

PART IV

PLAYING IN THE INTUITIVE FIELD

CHAPTER 9

SPEAKING THE LANGUAGE

The soul becomes dyed with the color of its thoughts.
— MARCUS AURELIUS

Now that we recognize all the moving parts of our First Intelligence, it is time to set the pieces in active and directed motion. But before we do that, let me share a powerful example of how the attributes and aspects of First Intelligence came together to provide the perfect guidance and the ideal outcome for a personal life adventure I was determined to take. As I tell the story, I will highlight specific intuitive facets as they take place, so that you can begin to recognize how the various attributes of intuition work together to create a positive and seemingly magical outcome.

I invite you to recall a similar experience in your life. It is important as you learn the language to precisely identify how similar experiences may have felt or otherwise made themselves known to you. The more specifically you identify your particular intuitive style, the easier it will be for you to recognize, trust, and follow the information you receive in the future.

CHOCOLATE CAKE AND THE SHAMAN

I can't tell you precisely *when* it hit me, nor can I *describe* the moment when I recognized the desire to do spiritual medicine work with a Peruvian shaman. I'd had an inkling of it for some time, but one day the desire reached critical mass and became tangible instead of ethereal.

To be specific, I felt called to do ceremonial work with the medicinal plant ayahuasca, and I wanted to do this work with a *curandero*, or shaman, who was meticulously schooled in the world of this ancient medicine. I didn't want to do it with some weekend spiritual warrior who for fun on a Saturday night invites a group of friends to come over and drink magic tea. My intention was to do it correctly, with someone who had deep reverence for the power of the work and saw it as part of a spiritual journey.

A few days after I acknowledged this desire, I told my roommate what I was thinking of doing. We had not discussed it before; she thought the idea was cool and we left it at that.

Intuitive facet in action: recognition of desire (see chapter 7, page 100).

Later that week my roommate received an invitation from a friend who had a friend whose other friend was premiering a documentary film about shamans of the Amazon and their amazing healing techniques using ayahuasca with people from all over the world. She extended the invitation to me, intrigued by the fact that we had just discussed it. We agreed to go.

The shamans believe that when it is time for someone to work with the ayahuasca medicine, the plant itself creates a graceful way for them to connect with it. The film reaffirmed my desire, and later that night I made a conscious choice, saying to myself, "I don't know how, but I am going to do this work with a shaman."

Intuitive facet in action: conscious acknowledgment and empowered choice (see chapter 7, page 101).

In my limited perspective at the time, the only way this could happen was the way it happened in the movie, and that meant I would have to get myself to the Amazon. As far as I knew, there were no highly trained shamans who specialized in ayahuasca medicine advertising in the Los Angeles phone book.

"Making" Things Happen

With my desire acknowledged and the choice made, I started in on the kind of outward and logical machinations that most people undertake in order to set off on an adventure of this magnitude.

Over the next several weeks, I researched the retreat centers in the area of the Amazon known to have the most legitimate and powerful shamans. I investigated affordable airfares, debated about the best time of year to go, got price quotes on hotels and other accommodations, corresponded with tour directors, and asked as many logical questions as I could come up with, including what shots I would need in order to travel to the Amazon and how long it would take to renew my passport. I did all the practical homework people usually do when planning for a long-distance vacation.

Finally content with one of the options, I made arrangements to send in the deposit to hold my space and tried to figure out how I was going to come up with the five thousand dollars and the three weeks' travel time required.

Tweak, push, cajole, and maneuver.

My mind spun for weeks. I admit there were even a couple of nights that I lost sleep over it. My main concern was that I had other financial obligations that took precedence over my flying to a jungle halfway around the world to play with some medicine men. But I knew there really *was* something to this calling, and I knew that one way or another I was going to answer it.

Noticing Resistance

When the day came for me to send five hundred dollars to hold my spot for the October retreat, I just couldn't do it. No matter what I said to convince myself that a delay would force me to miss my opportunity, I simply could not bring myself to mail the check. I'd go numb every time I would head to the post office, and I would feel a wall of energy blocking me.

Intuitive facet in action: recognizing resistance (see chapter 15, page 219).

The resistance was too powerful to ignore. I had felt signals from my intuition before and had paid a price when I ignored them. So, knowing better this time, I didn't send the check. "What the heck?" I thought. The desire was still there, but for some reason my body was telling me *this* particular action was not appropriate. I was supposed to hold on to my money. I had to trust that feeling, so without knowing precisely why, I let go of the idea of traveling to Peru.

Hit Me

The next day, the thought of an old friend named Eddie popped into my head. Eddie was the kind of person who was always smiling, and he had an energy about him that made him appear to shimmer. And there he was, hanging out in a shiny little thought-bubble in my mind.

Intuitive facet in action: inner vision/clairvoyance (see chapter 13, page 189).

I had not seen or spoken to Eddie in several years, and I had no current contact information for him. I did know he had been traveling the world doing business, and that he had recently gotten married, but that was all I knew of his life at the moment. Yet there he was, all clear and sparkly in my mind's eye. "Interesting," I thought as I noticed that I noticed the idea of Eddie. I didn't give it any weight; I simply recognized that this image of Eddie had gotten my attention.

My musing about whether I would ever get the chance to work with the shamans continued, as did the thought that perhaps I had made a big mistake by not sending in my deposit.

The Hits Keep Coming

The evening after I suddenly thought about Eddie, I was winding down at the end of the day and catching up on my emails, when the idea of "cake" flashed into my head. It was 8:30 at night, I was cozy in my bed and not particularly hungry, and I was not planning on going anywhere at this hour. Yet the cake impression was one I couldn't ignore.

Intuitive facet in action: inner hearing (clairaudience)/inner tasting (clairgustance) (see chapter 13, pages 190 and 194).

It could be considered passive, direct, and asynchronous (see chapter 13, pages 185, 186, and 187).

My favorite cake in the world is served at a restaurant near my home called the Alcove, and their chocolate Bundt cake is simply out of this world. If I thought I could get away with it, I would eat it for every meal.

For a moment I tried to talk myself out of the idea, but the power of the word *cake* had gotten my taste buds excited and I could already taste the thick fudge frosting. Resistance was futile.

"What the heck?" I thought. "Cake sounds good."

Let 'Em Eat Cake

So at 8:45 on a Tuesday night, dressed in my grubby sweatpants and a baseball cap, I jumped in my car to go get a piece of my favorite decadence. When I arrived at the restaurant, there was a line out the door.

"Crap," I thought, "I don't want to wait in this line," and for half a second I considered turning around and going home. But the thought "cake" flashed in my mind again, so I decided that since I had nothing better to do at this moment I would tough it out and wait for my slice of chocolate heaven.

As I stood in line, I noticed a man sitting by himself at a table near the checkout counter. It took me a moment to realize it, but when my eyes focused I couldn't believe it: that man was Eddie!

I quickly walked over to his table and greeted him with a hug. As we caught up, Eddie mentioned that he was in town for only a couple of days. He and his wife, Nicole, were packing up their old house, which was about two blocks away, and they were preparing for a move to Ojai, a couple of hours north.

When he asked what I was up to, I mentioned that I had thought of him the day before, and that I had been trying to navigate this desire to work with the shamans and was frustrated. I mentioned as well my concerns about the time and money it would take and the fact that I would have to travel alone, halfway around the world, to make it happen.

He smiled a knowing smile and said, "Well, Simone, you know as well as I do there are no accidents."

"Why do you say so?" I asked as I smiled back at him. I could feel the magic starting to solidify, and I got goose bumps all over.

Intuitive facet in action: physical response (see chapter 1, page 17).

"Nicole and I are hosting a gathering of friends in Malibu who will share a weekend with us and a very special man from Peru! He is a gifted shaman with a long family history, and he will share his practice and his wisdom with us."

There was a brief pause, and the smile on Eddie's face grew even larger. "Would you like to join us?"

Intuitive facet in action: path of least resistance (see chapter 8, page 132).

Fruition

A few days later I was seated on the floor in a room with about thirty people, sharing, listening, laughing, and learning from the heart of this lovely, gifted, and highly respected teacher. Wise and kind, funny and handsome, he spoke eloquently through a Spanish interpreter and awed us all with his words of healing and power. The experience left a mark on my soul, not only because of the power of the work itself, but also because of the way it had magically come into being.

In the days following this meeting with José (I have worked with him twice more), I felt the pull of Peru beginning to fade. The belief that I needed to travel halfway around the world and invest a large amount of time, effort, and money to work with a true medicine man had been erased by an experience, guided by intuition, that had unfolded easily, elegantly, and efficiently.

My desire had been deeply and profoundly fulfilled, but not in the way that I had *thought* it would be. I received what I wanted: the experience of studying with a gifted and magical shaman. My desire had become reality, and it had cost me only the price of a single piece of cake, which, as I recall, I wasn't even hungry for when I got home from my trip to the restaurant to buy it. The sheer simplicity of this story reshaped how I approach using First Intelligence in my own life and how I teach the language of intuition to others.

At the core of the story is the understanding that there is wisdom and intelligence unfolding around us at all times — and that intuition is, and always has been, responding to the thoughts we are thinking at any given moment in time. If we are to take advantage of this source of guidance, our task is to become aware of how we energetically occupy space within the field of intelligence and to learn to fine-tune, focus, and direct our energy so we can be more certain about how our intuition will respond to us when we make requests of it.

Intuition is simply a form of energetic conversation between mind and heart, body and soul, so if you are ready, it's time to get this conversation started.

CHAPTER 10

STEP 1:
GENERATING COHERENCE

The way is not in the sky. The way is in the heart.

— BUDDHA

As we discussed earlier, coherence is the energetic function of peace that supports every facet of our intuitive intelligence, empowering each aspect of our biological and energetic nature to operate and cooperate at peak levels. It amplifies and refines our ability to perceive the information held within the field that is in creative alignment with the outcome we desire.

Our intention in step 1 is to reduce if not eliminate all the distorted energies that place limitations on our ability to intuitively perceive information and to integrate all our biological and energetic intelligence systems so that they will work together as a balanced and harmonic whole.

Coherence balances and integrates

- all three parts of the Trilateral Intelligence System (brain, heart, gut);

- all three levels of the mind (superconscious, conscious, and subconscious); and
- all four levels of intuitive awareness (gut instinct, heart wisdom, visionary power, and connection to universal wisdom).

The foundation of peace that is established by a solid field of coherent energy supports all these physical, mental, and spiritual facets and brings them into alignment to activate and direct the intuitive conversation.

Using Our Inner Light

If we regard the impulse of a desire as a seed that must be planted if we are to bring an oak tree into being, then we should consider the power of coherence as being akin to the constantly flowing energy of the sun. It is the energy that activates the spark within the energetic seed of our desire. Without it, new creation of any kind cannot come to fruition.

This elevated and refined energy clarifies our perceptions, working its alchemical magic. It is like the heat used in refining metals to burn off the impurities, leaving only pure gold.

Cultivating Peace

I encourage you to designate a special place in your home as your intuitive working space. Just as you might have a special place to go when you exercise or work at home, this will be the quiet and private space you go to every day specifically to cultivate your intuitive practice.

Ideally, this practice would be a regular part of your day, like brushing your teeth or taking a shower. Consider starting and ending your day with fifteen minutes of focused coherence; gradually you will begin to notice a consistent increase in your sense of well-being and in the power of your intuition. Most likely, you will feel so good during the practice that you'll want to make it a longer part of your routine.

Eventually the feelings of peace will become habitual, memorized by your body and subconscious mind, and you will find yourself constantly enveloped in this active field of information. It will become the way you are every moment, and as a result you will have continual access to your intuition

Mother Teresa was known to say, "Peace starts with a smile." Intuitively she knew what the scientists have proven: that the simple act of smiling activates a multitude of beneficial hormones and neurotransmitters that lower blood pressure, stimulate neural pathways linked to happiness, ease pain, balance brain and body functions, and stimulate joy.

The following simple exercise will generate the coherent energies of peace and begin to balance and align all physical, mental, emotional, and spiritual attributes of your being. It will also harmonize those systems within the field of intelligence and information.

This meditation is not about going so deep within yourself that you shut down and get lost. Our intention is to remain peacefully aware of what we are doing and to be engaged in what we are experiencing while remaining receptive. This is what cultivating "an active peace" means.

EXERCISE
GENERATING COHERENCE

Close your eyes. Sit up straight so your spine is erect but relaxed. Find a position that allows you to be engaged with your body but not strained or uncomfortable in any way. Take a few deep breaths to release any tension you may feel in your body.

Sit for a few moments and feel the energetic vibration of

your body without doing anything. Simply notice what you notice. Noticing your noticing is an important part of your intuitive practice, and this is an easy and elegant way to begin.

You may notice a buzz, a feeling of opening, a vibration or bodily tingle; it may be very subtle or quite pronounced, and either way is fine. This subtle or pronounced buzz is the electrical field that all your cells and the DNA within them are using to communicate with one another and with the environment, both locally and nonlocally.

Now, with your eyes still closed, cultivate a deep, inner smile, one that moves from your face and into your heart. If it helps to place your hand over your heart to help you focus and isolate this area, then do so.

Gently say to yourself. "Peace. Peace. Peace." Continue to observe what is happening in your body without having to control it. Let your breath fall into its own natural pattern.

Focusing on the space around your heart, cultivate the gentle feelings of gratitude, appreciation, and care. Find something in your life that you can feel grateful for, or think of someone or something you care for.

Now gently bring to mind the feelings that you consider life affirming, and allow them to fill your heart. Feelings such as ease, grace, flow, confidence, certainty, expansion, abundance, and joy can and will assist you in further amplifying your energy.

Allow yourself to just soak in this feeling for a minute or two. Continue observing what you notice in your body.

From this point of activated peace, you have generated a coherent energy that has quieted all the habitual patterns and discordant functions of the lower mind that stand in the way of your expanded perceptions. Continue to sustain this calm yet elevated feeling for a few more minutes. Become intimate with this feeling, and begin to imprint it in your mind and body so you can shift back into it whenever you find yourself feeling out of sorts or stressed-out. This is the frequency and energy that I invite you to maintain all the time. Gently say to yourself, "This is my peace. This is my power. I will remember it."

Now without shifting, or letting go of this energy, open your eyes and come back into the world. Observe your surroundings and notice the expansion of your senses.

With enough practice you will be able to generate this feeling at will, and when you bump up against things that would normally cause stress, anger, or frustration, you will not be so easily swung out of place like that old pendulum "Bob."

What you have just done is settle into the frequency of peace that lacks the distortions, static blocks, and kinks that keep you from connecting to your higher mind. This process has already begun changing how your body and mind perceive the environment, and it has activated the level of mind function needed to precisely engage with the field that holds the intuitive intelligence we need.

An MP3 recording of this meditation is available on my website, www.simonewright.com.

CHAPTER 11

STEP 2:
ACCESSING THE FIELD

Out beyond the ideas of wrong doing and right doing, there is a field. I will meet you there.

— RUMI

Now the real work and the real fun begin. This is where we put in motion everything we have learned about the physical and energetic processes of our intuitive intelligence. There is still much to learn and understand, and those things will unfold as we progress.

As a soul possessing a mind and a body, we operate and exist in an entirely electromagnetic environment. And, as we know, we are made more of empty space than of solid matter. So it would be true to say that everything we are, and all we have experienced, is an energetic idea more than a material fact.

Our bodies are made up of more than 100 trillion cells. Our organs, bones, tissue, glands, and nerves each possess their own electromagnetic field of consciousness, operating in another, larger electromagnetic field of consciousness. Each cell expresses its energetic idea of self as a mathematical equation, or code, or what we might simply call an energetic fingerprint.

In the language of intuition, we call it vibration or resonance.

Researchers have hypothesized that there may be as many as 1.2 million different resonances happening in a human body at the same time. When perceived as a whole, they form a single energetic diagram of a unique individual.

Every car, rock, tree, horse, piece of jewelry, building, amoeba, or idea has its own unique electromagnetic fingerprint that is part of the unified field. And because the field operates like a recording medium, the energetic fingerprint of everything, past, present, or future, living or dead, is held in the field forever.

Even events have their own energetic fingerprints, which is how a psychic or intuitive is able to gather information from the field to assist a client with a concern or to find a solution to a crime for a police department. It may not seem like a stretch of the imagination to suppose that an intuitive could gather information about a past event, but how would he gain information about a future event? And how can we use the science involved in this process to cultivate our destiny?

THE INTUITIVE EARTH

Just like every other material experience, future events possess a unique and measurable energetic signal. Proof of this statement can be found in the Global Coherence Initiative, a research project undertaken by the Institute of HeartMath, which directly measures fluctuations in the magnetic fields generated by the earth and in the surrounding ionosphere.[1]

Their research reveals that the earth's magnetic field often changes weeks ahead of an earthquake or a volcanic eruption, and that the signals preceding these events can be measured. Researchers engaged in the Global Coherence Initiative accurately predicted the eruption of Mount St. Helens, and in the years following the original cataclysm they predicted over 80 percent of seismic activity occurring around a single detector in the vicinity.

The institute also monitored and evaluated measurements in the days and weeks surrounding the death of Princess Diana, on August 31, 1997, and the attacks on the World Trade Center and the Pentagon on September 11, 2001. Their findings indicated a major spike in stressors around the planet, and that the earth herself was responding electromagnetically to the emotional trauma that virtually the entire population was feeling during and after these planetary events. But what was most powerful, especially in regard to our work with intuition, was that the amplification of the stressors was noted several hours *before* the events, which suggests a global and collective intuition about what was about to happen.

Animals, too, are acutely sensitive to shifts in the earth's magnetic fields, as was powerfully exhibited during the catastrophic tsunami in Indonesia in December 2004. The devastation claimed over 250,000 human lives, but virtually no animal loss was reported.

In a stunning example of animal precognition, all the elephants at the Khao Lak Trekking Center broke free from their chains, ignoring the commands of their keepers, and ran for higher ground, some of them with tourists still strapped to their backs, more than five minutes before the wall of water made landfall. Animals of all kinds quickly moved away from the shoreline long before the wave was even visible. People all over the region who were responsible for animal welfare or caring for wildlife in sanctuaries and zoos reported that the loss of animal life was virtually nil and that in a village that lost three thousand humans, not a single animal perished.[2]

With no logical, rational, thinking mind to contradict the intuitive data gathered from the field, the animals did what they knew to do to survive. Most never returned to the lowland.

The Institute of HeartMath has proven that for humans as well, changes in the earth's magnetic field cause major shifts in the brain and nervous system. These shifts are often noted as alterations in memory, mood, or athletic or mental performance, as well as an increased sensitivity in a range of extrasensory perception experiments. The researchers note that in some cases in which people say they "feel" an oncoming earthquake or drastic weather change, their brain waves and heart rhythms are synchronized with the electromagnetic field of the planet and the subjects are reacting to the physical signals they perceive before the event. Whether these people take any sort of preemptive action is unknown.[3]

These experiments and natural phenomena prove that we are biologically aware of invisible yet measurable forces that can and do predict future events. The animals that survived the tsunami recognized the energetic fingerprint of the event and took immediate, lifesaving action.

The benefit for us as conscious beings with free will is that we can link with this field using our own biology, not to access a predetermined or fated future, but to gain information about an event of our choosing — an event we would like to experience, a future opportunity we would be grateful to participate in, one that would change our lives and our futures for the better.

ENERGETIC FINGERPRINTS

Each of the tragic events that I just discussed has a unique electromagnetic code now stored within the unified field. Akin to a mathematical formula, this energetic fingerprint is a complete and holographic picture, with the details, seen and unseen, known and unknown, that make up the whole.

Developing your intuition is meant to empower you, not so you can know what *might* happen in your future, but so you can use it to guide yourself into a future you have *chosen* and designed for yourself.

Every idea, every solution, every problem, every health issue, every crime, every relationship, every wealthy life, and every impoverished one has its own individual and unique frequency. Your job is to use the power of your will and focus to generate an energetic feeling state aligned with the peaceful vibrations associated with the solution to that situation. This energetic alignment allows you to enter the field and gather as much information as you need in order to move closer to that outcome.

When I work on a police investigation without knowing the outcome and details, the only energetic item I can bring to that situation is my intention. In most cases, regardless of the circumstances, this is "an intention to discover the truth." With that intention clearly set, I then instruct my intuitive mind to bring forward the information that is aligned with that truth. Truth in a situation that has already occurred has a specific vibratory code or frequency, and often the simple intention to link with this frequency is enough to discover information that helps move the investigation forward.

If you are intuitively working on a situation about which you would simply like to know as much pertinent information as possible, setting the intention "Show me the truth" — and using your new ability to generate coherence, and feeling the feeling of appreciation for the answer — is a powerful way to begin.

But in a situation in which we want to use intuition to guide us to a circumstance that we deliberately *want* to create, we align ourselves with the energetic code by starting at the end. That is to say, because we know that the solution or beneficial outcome already exists within the field of all possibilities, in order to connect to those bits of information we must generate and amplify all the feelings of having our desire already achieved, our solution already discovered, our result already garnered, our prayer already answered.

This part of the work is an aspect of *precision* and, simply stated, is like punching your destination address into the GPS of your car.

If you want to get to San Francisco, you won't get there if you enter a New York address. In order for the combined power of your conscious, subconscious, and superconscious minds to align and work toward a common goal, you must know what that goal is and you must stick to it, lest you give the different aspects of mind mixed signals.

THE POWER OF CHOICE

What do you want to create? What problem do you want to solve? What desire do you want to fulfill? What goal do you want to achieve? What do you want to heal? What outcome do you want to generate?

What you desire may be to heal an illness. To become wealthy. To create or improve a relationship. To find a new job or expanded place of purpose. To own a new car. To lose weight. To find a lost piece of jewelry. To have a new home or place to live. It does not matter, nor is any one desire more noble than any other. If you have a desire of any kind, consider it a whisper from the mind of creation calling you higher and asking you to make greater use of your creative faculties. Discard any judgment or superstition that the desire to have improved material expression in your life is petty, selfish, or nonspiritual. When you know the true laws of the mind, you know that you can and will generate the outcome you desire without prohibiting anyone else from having what they desire.

Empowered choice is the spark that gets the potential energy held within the creative field fired up. You *must* make a choice; otherwise you will remain stuck in neutral, and the power of the law of averages and the group mind will take over and you will continue to live the same life you have always lived. Choose to be successful and mean it, and you will be. Choose to be healthy and mean it, and you will be.

Remember when I said earlier that living intuitively is not

for sissies? This is where faith, trust, and courage come into play, because at this moment of choice you must believe that you have what it takes to make the wisest decision for your life, and that come hell or high water it *will* be the best decision you have ever made.

As we saw when we discussed the cycle of the intuitive mind, the divine superpower of the conscious mind is the ability to *choose*. Any choice driven by certainty and commitment carries within it an electrical charge that activates the creative process simply by virtue of its power and begins the process of carving the chosen desire out of the field of all possibility.

Have you ever experienced a moment in your life when you were sick and tired of going through the same frustrations or situations over and over, and one day you just said to yourself, "I am done with this nonsense! I cannot, will not, am not going to do it anymore!" and things seemed to suddenly transform for you? Or conversely, was there a time when you decided you really *did* want to do something, and you made a choice that sounded like: "I don't know how I'm going to do it, but I'm going to get my degree, lose fifty pounds, take a trip to Africa, and start my own business."

It didn't matter whether other people said you were insane. In that moment you meant it for *real*, and things happened to help make your choice a reality. This is an instance of the energetic charge of empowered choice setting things in motion in the field. But you have to really mean it. A soft or wimpy choice will not work. We have all made halfhearted choices, and we ended up saying, when it came down to taking action: "Eh, I'll start tomorrow." Then we sat down in front of the TV and nothing changed.

Soft choices happen when we worry about what other people might think about us. They happen when we believe that our age, or our bank balance, or our gender has more power than our soul does. Soft choices happen when we don't believe, for whatever reason, that what we are saying could truly happen. We say it to ourselves, or maybe even say it aloud to someone else, but we don't mean it, not really, and life stays the same.

Empowered choice is the starting point for all creative action. It is the jump start that the subconscious mind needs in order to turn possibility into actuality. Remember what the unified field shows us, that mind must be present in order for anything to "be" at all. An empowered choice, one that is focused on a clear intention, acts like a laser beam, causing all subjective possibilities that exist at any given moment within the field to collapse into a singular objective reality.

When you make a true, empowered choice, your subconscious snaps out of its programmed routine as if to say, "Wow, she is really serious. I might have to pay attention to her this time." Think of it being like a family taking a road trip. The two kids are in the back, doing what kids do on road trips: they are irritating each other. They tickle, prod, bug, overstep the middle boundary line, and give each other wet willies. Mom says from the front seat, "Cut it out, kids." But the kids continue poking at each other. "Stop it, kids." The torture continues. "Knock it off, you guys." It goes on. And then Mom explodes at them, shouting, "I mean it, you guys. *Knock it off!*"

The amplified charge in Mom's attitude captures the kids' attention. They stop what they are doing and follow her orders. Every once in a while they may flare up again, and Mom has to remind them of what she wants them to do, but they have gotten the message.

This is precisely the relationship between our conscious and subconscious minds. It isn't enough to tell the subconscious just once; the communication has to continue. But an empowered choice at the very beginning is enough to get the process rolling. The moment of powerful choice making does not have to be a rare occasion; it can become a regular phenomenon in your life if you know how and why you are doing it.

Choose bravely. Choose clearly. Choose with eyes forward and head held high. Choose with the power of one who is imbued with all the creative capacity of the universe. Choose as one who is making a decree, setting a new law, or establishing a new precedent in your life. You, as ruler of your world, have made a decision — it is supported, it is correct, and it is your divine right.

Your choice must have enough power behind it that

1. it captures the attention of the subconscious mind; and
2. it is strong enough to overpower any subconscious pattern that may have been running in the past.

The mind will follow the direction of the thought or belief that has the most power, not necessarily the one that makes the most sense.

EXERCISE
IT'S YOUR CHOICE

In your notebook, write down as many things as you can think of that you choose to create. Let your imagination flow, without editing. What do you choose to heal? What do you choose to improve? What do you choose to release? What do you choose to reveal? What do you choose to develop?

After you have made your list, select one goal or desire. You can work on additional creations later. Circle it. Based on whatever goal you have chosen, state clearly to yourself, silently or aloud, an empowering phrase that aligns with that goal. Examples of these power statements might be: I choose to be wealthy. I choose to be in the perfect job for me. I choose to be at my ideal weight. I choose to have a healthy relationship. I choose to be successful. I choose to write my first screenplay. I choose to experience love. I choose to step forward with joy. I choose to deepen my relationship with the divine. The choice is entirely up to you, but whatever it is, mean it as if your future life depends on it...because it does.

FORM AND FUNCTION

Now that you have chosen what you want, you must align yourself with the field of information so the power of your elevated consciousness knows where to look for the information. Remember what we discussed earlier: our intuition doesn't actually go anywhere; the information is constantly surrounding us, but we must tune our mind to the information we seek so our mind can pluck it from the field.

As I mentioned before, every situation, solution, person, success, failure, or problem has its own code, a source of energetic information that provides the foundation for it to be manifested in the material realm. What we see in our reality, or our physical world, is the densest or slowest-moving form of that energetic code.

A great analogy that explains this concept is water. Water has an energetic source code that begins in the higher energetic realms of creation. We experience ice as the densest representation of that energy; liquid water is less dense. Steam is less dense than liquid water; vapor is less dense than steam; molecules of H_2O are less dense than vapor; atoms are less dense than molecules; and subatomic particles are less dense than atoms. After that, all we are left with is energy, which ultimately leads us back to the source code. All these stages of water represent different forms of the same energetic base material. The more slowly the foundational energies move, the denser they appear in our physical reality. The product we know as *ice*, for example, is considered the *form* of a higher originating energy.

When we use our intuition to find a solution for us, the final outcome — the achieved goal, the solved crime, the saved marriage, the recovered child, or the financial success — is the form. The universal field does not understand or communicate in form or have any understanding of money, weight, a new house, relationships, or any of that physical stuff. The only language the field understands is that of energy or vibration. It speaks a language of function.

To use another analogy, that of listening to the radio: if we want to listen to the station KSOUL, KSOUL is the form. It is what we want to hear when we turn the dial. But the signal that our radio sends out so it can pick up that radio station is not the letters *KSOUL* but rather an energetic, electromagnetic frequency that represents or symbolizes the call letters *KSOUL*. This frequency is sent out into the energetic field, where it connects to the waves within the field that provide our radio with the information coming from the KSOUL station.

The call letters of the radio station constitute form, but in order to transmit and receive information from the field we must communicate using function. *Function* is the vibrational frequency, or the energy that we put out into the field in order to gain our intuitive information. Generating this frequency is another important aspect of *precision* in the intuition triad.

The function of anything is the energetic code, or fingerprint, that is used by life to generate forms in the physical realm. It is the emotional, energetic feeling that we generate when we experience or perceive the solved problem, the answered prayer, or the created outcome.

If you want to use intuition to help you find a new job, you need to access the field via the energy of having that perfect job, the one that is suited to your highest potential now. Enter the field with that feeling of security. Enter the field knowing that you are well paid and doing what you love. Enter the field knowing that you are living in your perfect situation. Enter through the energies of satisfaction, confidence, and certainty.

You must enter the field with the understanding that the power of your higher mind sees solutions that your limited perspective does not have access to, and that this power is preparing to offer them to you with perfect timing.

Or to use a more extreme example, if I were called to help find a missing child and bring him home, I would need to enter the energetic field by generating the frequency of the completed goal, which is that the child is brought home. The tricky part of this particular instance is that at the outset we may not know whether that child is dead or alive, which ultimately I can hold no opinion about. If we find the child alive, then we have been successful and he is returned home. And even if we find the child deceased, the outcome, while devastating, is the same: he is still returned home.

Regardless of the outcome, I must enter the field knowing that the superconscious aspect of me, which is not separate from me, knows more than the "little me" does and can see solutions, opportunities, ideas, and possibilities that I am not aware of. Nothing is lost, unknown, or unsolvable to the superconscious mind. It is my job to stay aligned with the energies of the successful goal so that my intuitive wisdom will have clear access to my conscious mind, which is ready and waiting to receive the information.

GENERATING THE CODE

The energetic code found at the foundation of creation is based on the frequency of feeling. We want to achieve or create things not for the *things'* sake but rather for how they will make us feel and for the energies that they will allow us to experience because they are part of our lives. Some examples:

- Having more money might create the feelings of security, well-being, accomplishment, and freedom.
- Finding a spouse might create the feelings of security, love, comfort, and a sense of belonging or connection.

- Healing a disease might create the feelings of ease, vitality, joy, and freedom.

All these feelings are the functions of the forms we want to see in our world. The function is the *spiritual* aspect; and the form is the *material* aspect. And just to remind you, *mind* is the middle point between the two.

Take a closer look at the energies that are all listed as a final outcome: security, well-being, connection, joy, belonging. If you go deeper into the foundations of these energies, what do you notice? Ultimately the energy you will find underlying all of them is peace.

So using the single choice that you circled earlier on your list in the exercise "It's Your Choice" (page 156) please write out all the energetic *functions* (feelings) you can think of that you would experience if you had already achieved your successful outcome. The more feelings you can identify, the better. Once you have identified these energetic outcomes, take a few moments to notice the common energy that underlies them all. Make this discovery personal and meaningful for yourself. Do your best to truly recognize this base frequency, whatever it appears to be to you, because this will be the "source code" you use to access all the information you need from the field.

How would you identify your source code? Please write it down. This is the energetic function, or the spiritual aspect, of your goal.

This source code is specific to you and *your* answer, solution, or goal. Even if two people want to create the same things or they have the same problem to solve, the codes for each of them will be different based on the tiny differences in their emotions, beliefs, and attitudes about the situation in particular and about life in general. This is why no two people's solutions are exactly the same, and why counting on anyone else to find solutions for you is not as potent as your discovering them for yourself.

At this point you have two of the aspects of mind activated: your conscious mind is holding the *mental* choice of outcome that you made, and your subconscious mind has been activated and opened by the amplification of the heart frequencies vibrating in alignment with the *emotional* choice of your outcome. This combination of electromagnetic forces produced by the brain and heart is the code that is being sent into the field to link to the intuitive information you need in order to move toward your goal.

Meditate on this feeling and frequency for a few minutes, so that you can feel it becoming natural, normal, and organic for you. Eventually it will become a frequency you can maintain at all times and one that you will use as your base frequency for everything you do. When this becomes a habitual pattern, you will have constant and direct access to your intuition in every moment of the day, and you won't have to set aside a specific time to work on it, unless you want to.

At the same time that you are generating this coherent field of energy from your heart (emotional choice), you must activate the mental choice by using the imaginative power of the conscious mind and directing it to your image of the future outcome.

REMEMBERING THE FUTURE

In chapter 3, we discussed the unified field, and I had you do a memory exercise about something you had experienced in the past. Remember how easy it was to do that? And remember where that memory was stored? Now we are going to use that same process to "remember the future."

When you use the imaginative power of your conscious mind to craft the outcome that you have solved the problem, found the solution, or cultivated the destiny, begin with the thought "I remember..."

If you want to use your intuition to guide you toward getting a new car, enter this part of the process with: "I remember buying my new car." Then play that scenario out as a memory.

If you want to use it to guide you to getting married, enter the process with: "I remember the day I walked down the aisle." Then play it out as a memory.

If you have lost something important and need to find it, enter the process with: "I remember the moment I found my lost (ring, key, wallet). Then play it out as a memory.

If you want to use it to help you heal a certain illness, enter the process with: "I remember the day my doctor told me I was perfectly healthy." Then play that out as a memory.

Our intuition *cannot* guide us to anything we are *not* already conscious of. The more we train our mind to perceive the future outcome as something that has already happened (which, as we know, exists as a possibility within the field), the more readily the subconscious mind will use its power of compulsive creativity to help bring it about.

There is a subtle yet powerful difference between past and future mind states. They both have the ability to influence the subconscious mind, but "remembering the future" seems to have greater impact when you're trying to gather intuitive information from the field more quickly. The mind is doing the same thing in both processes — that is, it's focusing on a certain event held within the field. The only difference is the feeling of certainty and calm aligned with treating it as a memory rather than a possibility.

EXERCISE
CREATING YOUR FUTURE

Use your imagination to cultivate the visions, ideals, and possibilities of the "who you would be" if your destiny were already a done deal. Imagine what you would be doing with the outcome already achieved. How would you be behaving if your prayer were already answered? Where would you be if your problem were already solved? What would your attitude be? How would you feel emotionally? What would you look like? How would you spend your time? How would you spend your money? Who would be with you? What sort of conversations would you be having?

Play this scenario out as fluently as possible, with as much detail as you can muster. Play it out in your mind as if you are *remembering a past experience.*

Allow yourself to meditate with the complete emotional, mind, and heart frequency for five to ten minutes, or more. As you do this exercise, you alter your own electromagnetic field, so that every cell and strand of DNA works as a coherent unit to act as a biological antenna to energetically link you to the information you seek. Make it as real and juicy and natural as possible. When you feel that you have become saturated with the energetic code, it is time to start asking for guidance and direction.

CHAPTER 12

STEP 3:
THE POWER OF THE "ASK"

For everyone who asks receives; the one who seeks finds; and to the one who knocks, the door will be opened.

— MATTHEW 7:7

In this step, we form a specific target question so that our intuition has a potent search command. The coherent frequencies of our source code, aligned with peace, have granted us access to the informational field that holds the intuitive intelligence we need. But equally vital to us now is *how* we engage with it once we have entered.

At this stage, we will once again use the directive power of the conscious mind to lead the subconscious to find the information we need. And then we will release it, or "hand it over," to the advanced power of the superconscious, which will work out the details. Here is where the conscious and subconscious minds "ask for directions," and the superconscious mind provides those directions for us.

In order to receive the information that is most applicable to our circumstance, we must ask questions that are mentally structured to align with the goal at hand. But they must also be energetically structured to align with the principles and ideals of the higher mind.

You may remember something I said earlier: if we want access to the powerful information stored in the kingdom of heaven, we cannot expect to find it hidden in the basement.

Becoming proficient at the "ask" requires a bit of consideration and practice, but once mastered it becomes an automatic function. Eventually it will work as quickly as thought.

There are potent and impotent ways to engage the field. There are questions that will align you and allow your intuition to move quickly and clearly, and there are questions that will create static in the field and cause the transfer of information to be distorted, incomplete, or nonexistent. The single most important question to ask yourself as you develop your questions is: "Is this ask empowered or disempowered?" Empowered questions will garner results; disempowered ones won't. Empowered questions increase your coherence and, in laser-like fashion, intensify your effectiveness as you seek more precise information.

POOR BEGINNINGS

I'm going to save you some time right away and remove from the list some of the questions you might consider using. Not because they are good or bad, or right or wrong, but simply because they are energetically ineffective.

The first question to eliminate from your intuitive toolbox: "Is there a solution to this problem?" Variations on this question might be: "Is there a way out?" or "Is there an answer?" There is *always* a solution, a way out, a way in, or a way through. This isn't a cliché; it is a principle of nature.

As we saw earlier when discussing peace, perception, and precision, inherent within the energetic footprint of every circumstance is the principle of polarity, which stipulates that the elements of both the problem and the solution exist within the whole. According to this principle, if the problem exists, so too does the solution; they differ from one another only in degree and in level of vibration. Consider approaching every situation with this thought: "I know there is a solution to every problem, and that my intuitive mind is directing me toward it now. What is my most appropriate first step?"

WHY ASK WHY?

The second group of questions I encourage you to remove from your inquiry list is the group that begin with *why*, such as: "Why is this happening?" "Why is this person behaving this way?" "Why can't I get this part of my life right?"

Why embodies the vibration of victimization and carries an energetic charge of helplessness or defeat. Reflect back on the times you have been in a difficult situation or crisis and asked the question of yourself, your friends, or the universe. You may have been so frustrated, tired, or broken that you dropped to your knees and shouted to God, your angels, or whoever might be listening, "*Why?*"

Why seeks a clarification, rationalization, or logical explanation for a situation; it does not seek wisdom or direction.

Intuition does not explain; it simply interprets information found in the field and translates it. If you are seeking a rationalization, which is a trademark of the limited lower mind, intuition will not help you. When we engage our First Intelligence, we do so to gain guidance from our higher mind; we want to know what *actions* to take so we can move forward in the most appropriate way. *Why* will not give us direction, nor will it move us forward. To keep the process of your work aligned with the foundational energy of precision, do not use *why*. A more empowered approach might be: "I know there is creative purpose in all things. How can I best use this circumstance to propel me forward?"

WHERE THERE'S A WILL

Another line of disempowered questioning is the one that begins with "Will I?" "Will I win the debate?" "Will I succeed at the proposal?" "Will I be happy? "Will I make the team?"

As we have already discovered, one of the most powerful aspects of being a conscious human being is having the ability to generate a potent field of energy that is activated by focused choice and imbued with the gift of will. If you *choose* to be happy, you will be. If you make an empowered choice to be successful, you will be. If you make a choice to be in a loving relationship, you will be.

Destiny is not random, nor is it fate; it happens by choice — choice guided by wisdom, trust, and courage. Learning to activate and rely on your First Intelligence requires all three of those things from you. Do not give up your ability to cocreate your life by placing the power of will or choice in the hands of someone else or by throwing it to the winds of chance. This will not serve you. A more empowered approach might be: "I know my choice has great power. What action can I take now to further empower this choice?"

SHOULD I?

The fourth group of questions to avoid begin with *should*. As in: "Should I get married?" "Should I take this job?" "Should I make this investment?" Questions that begin with *should* tend to be sourced by a desire to steer clear of risk and to gain a feeling of safety and certainty. We want to hear: "Yes, you should," to avoid making the wrong decision so we don't have to either risk feeling uncomfortable or push beyond too many boundaries.

Guidance aligned with our evolution often requires us to do things that may feel risky, and it often insists that we develop trust as we navigate through them. It will encourage us to take actions that press us to the limits of what have known in the past, so we must go to our heart to develop the courage we need to complete the task.

"Should I?" is a question of limitation, not a question of expansion. A more empowered statement might be: "I know my higher mind is leading me to the best outcome in this moment. What is the wisest choice to make at this time?"

STRUCTURING PRECISE POWER QUESTIONS

The following describe the dynamics of empowered and precise power questions:

1. They activate and use the conscious and subconscious aspects of the mind.
2. They focus on our current need, in the present moment.
3. They address a single concern at a time.
4. They provide direction.
5. They use the positive form of the question.

Let's use these parameters in the form of an example:

Whenever I see a celebrity psychic on television, and the host offers up the microphone for questions from the studio audience, invariably a woman in the audience asks, "Will I be married in the next year?" This line of questioning makes me cringe, because there is a huge bucket of energy behind that question that limits anyone's ability to clearly see whether the answer is yes or no, even if the psychic or intuitive is incredibly talented.

Here is how I would advise the woman who asks that question (this response may not be entertaining for television, but at least it may be more appropriate for her):

HER: "Will I be married in the next year?"

ME: "Would you like to be married?"

HER: "Yes."

ME: "Are you in a relationship now?"

HER: "No."

ME: "All right then. There is potential in all things and all desires. If you desire to create a loving relationship and are not in one now, there are things you should first ask, say, and do to create that for yourself; you should not be worrying about a wedding yet."

CHECKING THE DETAILS

Let's compare this woman's question — "Will I be married in the next year?" — to a precise power question and see how it holds up.

First we'll ask: does it actively use the conscious and subconscious aspects of the mind?

No. There is no *conscious* activation of the power of choice to make a declarative statement that directs the subconscious mind to find a creative solution. There is no energetic foundation of any sort to provide this woman with any guidance. In this example, she has taken her hands off the wheel of her life and is leaving her destiny up to chance, fate, and the law of averages.

Our second consideration: is it a current need, in the present moment?

Yes, it is a current need because she wants a relationship now. But it does not relate to the present moment, because she is projecting a year out. Timing is a tricky dimension to work in intuitively, and it depends entirely on the ability of the individual to focus her energy and remain clear of beliefs or attitudes that will interfere with her progress.

Our third consideration: is it focused on a single need?

Yes. The question is solely about marriage, which is good form. What many people tend to do is group their questions together, as in:

"Will I get married and have a baby?" or "Should I sell my house and buy a new one?" Keep the questions focused on a single need at a time. You can work on other questions individually as you begin to move forward, but remember: a radio cannot receive two stations at once.

Fourth: is it focused on providing direction?

No, It does not actively ask First Intelligence to provide a course of action or a pathway to achieving the goal. There is no opening here where intuition can tell the woman what to "do."

Fifth: is it focused on the positive form of the question?

It focuses on neither a positive nor a negative aspect. It is neutral in its energetic charge, which is better than being negative but doesn't offer any real precision. Our goal is to find a solution or a positive outcome, not to avoid an outcome we don't want. Do you see the difference? While the two outcomes may seem the same, the source energy for finding a solution is very different from the source energy for avoiding a problem.

Let's take a look at some paired questions and see if you can sense the difference between those that are empowered and those that aren't. The easiest way to tell the difference in the level of power in each question is to read them aloud and pay attention to how your body feels as you do so.

Notice that each question begins with a direction or statement from the conscious mind that sets the tone and directs the subconscious mind. In each question, pay attention to whether it is sourced in the ideals of the higher mind or of the lower mind. It should be obvious to you by now that our goal is to *always* work from the level of higher mind in order to benefit as much as possible from its wisdom and expanded perspective.

EMPOWERED OR NOT SO MUCH?

If you are facing a financial issue at work, which of the following two questions would be more helpful to ask:

I'm screwed. How am I going to make payroll?
What is the most potent step to take to immediately improve my cash flow?

If you are facing a personal financial issue, which question would you ask:

I can't make ends meet. How am I going to get out of debt?
There is an ideal solution available for me now. How can I begin to improve my finances right away?

If you are considering making a financial investment:

This is risky business. Am I going to make any money on this deal?
I know I am guided to make the best choice. Is this investment the wisest use of my money at this time?

If you need solutions to a health problem:

I am miserable. How do I stop feeling like crap?
I know I am meant to experience perfect health. What can I begin doing today that will improve my wellness?

If you have concerns about whether partnering with someone (personally or professionally) is in your best interests:

I really don't know what to do. Should I be worried about this guy?
I know there is a perfect outcome for me. Will a partnership with (the person's name) promote my highest good at this time?

Structuring the "ask" takes a bit of practice, but with time it will become second nature. As you become more intimate with the language of First Intelligence, it will become more automatic and natural. Eventually you won't even need to generate a question but will merely hold the thought of the situation you want directions for, and the solution or action will automatically appear.

A MATTER OF TIME

Time is one of the most difficult aspects for intuitive intelligence to nail down, especially because of the continuing expansion of consciousness. Time seems to be moving faster than ever before. For the purpose of determining the best timing of a certain issue, the following "ask" will work very well: Is the timing appropriate for me to take action/make a decision/move forward in the issue at hand? And remember to always start with the empowered-choice statement from the conscious mind: "I know that my intuitive mind is directing me to the perfect opportunity" (or a similar statement). Other "asks" that may be useful to you:

- Is the timing appropriate for me to start looking for a new job?
- Is the timing appropriate for me to submit my new book proposal?
- Is the timing appropriate for me to sell my home?
- Is the timing appropriate for me to expand my business?

Then, using your identification for *yes/no*, *safe/unsafe*, and so on, that you determined in the "Intuition Taste Test" exercise in chapter 5, notice what you notice, and base your actions on that impression.

Notice the specificity used in identifying the action and the issue at hand, and notice as well that the question is not "Is it the *right* time for me to sell my home?" "Right" or "wrong" is, once again, a judgment call based in the black-and-white logic of the rational mind. It is based in learning gleaned from past experience and makes no room for the creative flexibility required by our intuition. Your higher mind will guide you to what is most correct for you, or in your best interests at any given time, not what might be considered right or wrong by other standards.

Keep in mind that appropriate timing is based on a lot of things and has many moving parts, including the trajectories and life missions of other people. It is a waste of energy to try to force the timing of something, so if the impression you receive when you ask about timing is "No," don't stress out about it. Simply give it a week or so, until you feel guided to inquire, and then ask again. You will never miss out on any opportunity because of timing; there is always another bus to your destiny coming up the road. Trust that this is so.

BUILDING YOUR "ASK"

Now you are going to generate a precise power question to assist you in guiding you ahead in a chosen situation in your life. Such queries should be personal or related to you. Do not at this stage make inquiries for or about another person. Your precision at this time is not developed enough to engage in information gathering for someone else.

Please focus on only one situation at a time. In the beginning stages of this work, the minute signals of specific requests may energetically bump into one another and you will get your signals crossed, which will ensure no informational return at all. Do not rush the process; you will have plenty of time to work on many other important queries as you develop your skill.

Here are some examples of empowered-choice statements:

- I know the power of my intuitive mind has the perfect solution for me.
- I know that my higher mind knows exactly how to heal me.
- It is in my divine nature to experience abundance in all ways.
- My superconscious mind knows precisely how to make this a winning situation for everyone.

Can you come up with some more?

Here are some examples of potent power questions that can be linked to the preceding empowered-choice statements.

- What is the first thing I can do to grow my business?
- What can I do to cultivate more energy throughout my day?
- How can I be of greater value to my company? Family? Community?

- What career choice can I make today that will support my need for creativity?
- What foods would be most appropriate to help me lose weight?
- What does my child need from me to feel greater happiness?
- How can I heal my relationship with my spouse? Child? Parent? Friend?
- How can I present myself to the world in a way that is best suited to my essence?
- Is this car the wisest investment of my money?
- How I can be of greater service?
- What does my boss need from me to help our company succeed?

Can you see the commonality in them? Do you see how you might structure your own questions?

When I am working on a police investigation, I keep my "ask" specific and simple by stating to myself, "I know the truth is available to me. What happened here?" When I am looking for a missing child I say, "I know nothing is lost in the universal mind. Where is Jamie?" When I am working one-on-one with clients, especially if it is a new partnership, I always state, "I know there is a perfect outcome available. What is most important for Susan to know at this time?"

Then I surrender to the power of the superconscious mind and let my intuitive instrument run. Whatever is most significant to the work at hand is what is pops into my conscious awareness.

It doesn't have to be complicated. But as when learning a language or an artistic skill, you need to be a bit regimented at first and follow the guidelines so you have a solid foundation to build on. Eventually, when it becomes second nature, you can improvise and have a bit more fun.

PUTTING IT TOGETHER

Earlier, you crafted your choice of the current situation, circumstance, or outcome that you wanted your First Intelligence to work on. And you cultivated the source-code feeling that links you to the field. Here we get to practice precision once more. Hold the feeling of that situation in your body and mind for a moment and then write in one sentence what condition you want to change. What problem do you want to solve? What do you want answers for? Is it about money? Is it about health? Is it about a relationship? Is it about your job? Is it about your living situation?

What would you like the end result to be? Would you like to be twenty pounds lighter? Would you like to be completely debt-free? Would you like to have a wonderful new relationship? Would you like the perfect job? In one sentence, please write out your goal.

Keeping the five precision guidelines in mind:

1. Activate and use the conscious and subconscious aspects of the mind.
2. Focus on your current need in the present moment.
3. Address a single concern at a time.
4. Provide direction.
5. Use the positive form of the question.

Write out your ask. Remember to start with the conscious directive statement, then follow up with the question. Silently repeat the question to yourself two or three times. Notice if you feel expansion or contraction. If it feels appropriate for you, then stick with what you have crafted. If it feels off in some way, continue to restructure and energetically reinvestigate until it feels right/good/appropriate.

Hold the vision of the answered prayer or solved problem. Now quietly state your ask. It can be said aloud, or silently within your mind and heart. Repeat it gently several times. Once you have repeated it a few times, continue to maintain the coherent and peaceful energy of your source code and simply notice what you notice.

You can maintain this meditative process for as long as you like, but it is usually good to begin with at least ten minutes. Sometimes it takes a while for all the moving parts of your intuitive system to link up and entrain with one another.

LETTING IT GO

The final but crucial part of the process is releasing the ask to the power of the superconscious mind. This is the point in the intuitive process at which, energetically speaking, we surrender our request so that this elevated aspect of our consciousness can make things happen.

This is where all the magic occurs; this is where coincidences, synchronicities, brand-new creative ideas, and seemingly miraculous things are cultivated. We know that this level of mind knows the perfect way to provide the answer for us, and that when it is given, it will appear in a way that is geared to perfect right action. It will be perfectly suited to who we are in that moment, and it will be aligned with our highest good. When our intuitive guidance is aligned with these attributes, we know without doubt that we are one step closer to creating the outcome we desire.

To release the ask to the power of the superconscious mind, simply imagine the question being released into the air like a balloon or floating down a river like a toy boat. Then, at the end of your meditation, say, "I release this ask to the power of my higher mind. I know without a doubt that the perfect answer is available for me and is coming to me with perfect timing. Thank you."

That little expression of gratitude at the end is the energetic cherry on the sundae. It will open the door to your ability to receive. From this point on, your only job is to get on with your day and continue to maintain the coherent feeling of your answered prayer, and to start to notice what you notice.

GENERATING THE POWER TO RECEIVE

Activating our ability to receive is a crucial part of using our First Intelligence. In order for us to gain the greatest benefit from it, we must be open to *receiving* ideas and inspiration to direct us into new destinies. We must be willing to *receive* support, both energetically and physically, to help us move through the day. We must be able to *receive* guidance and information to lead us forward on our journey. When we can be open to this level of receiving and can use it to improve our lives, we can shift elegantly back into the energy of giving and use all we have gained to help, guide, and inspire others.

The truth of the matter is that most of us are very poor receivers, both in the energetic, intuitive way and in the material, physical way. The fact that one is material and one is spiritual does not matter; if there is a block to receiving, it will make itself known in both realms.

Two powerful yet misunderstood directives are common in today's New Age teachings. The first one says that it is better to *give* than it is to *receive*, and the second one says that in order to *receive* you need to go out and *give*. Both of these statements are incomplete and operate strictly on the limited understanding of the material world. So not only do they limit our ability to access the infinite and unbounded field of creation, but to a certain degree they also shame us for our desire to have wonderful things appear in our lives.

Working with the principle of polarity, we should understand that giving and receiving are but opposite polarities on a scale that could be considered the "exchange of energy." On one side of the scale is "giving." When we move up the scale by degrees, we find that on its other side is "receiving." All balanced aspects of nature are governed by this principle.

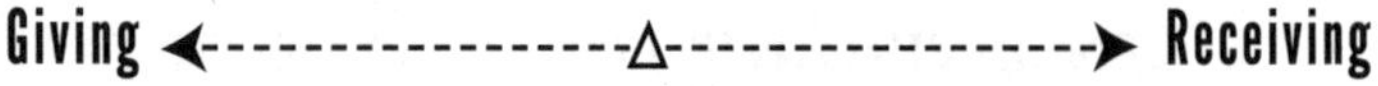

Giving ◄- - - - - - - - - - - - - - -△- - - - - - - - - - - - - - -► **Receiving**

Figure 17. The scale of energetic exchange

This scale is also present in our intuitive work. In order to *receive* the appropriate guidance, we must *give* the correct energy and we must *give* the correct request. Most of us have no problem with the giving aspect. But when it comes to receiving, we tend to have some trouble, often because of our own false beliefs about what it means to receive.

We do the giving work from our end, but an obstacle within us blocks our ability to benefit from our efforts. When this happens we tend to say, "This stuff doesn't work," or "I can't do it." This, of course, simply adds more weight to the already-loaded obstacle. And that makes it difficult not only to receive the information we wish to discover through our intuition but also to receive the benefits from the outcome we seek.

IDENTIFYING THE BLOCKS

To generate the power of receiving, we must first recognize the energetic blocks we carry that prevent us from moving forward on the scale of energetic exchange.

Considerations

- What, if any, negative feelings, beliefs, or attitudes do you have about receiving? Have you been taught that it is better to give than to receive? Are you able to receive *anything* with ease and grace? A compliment? Assistance? A gift? Advice?

- If you do receive these things, do you find yourself needing to justify, diminish, or limit the idea that you deserve them? For example, if someone gives you a compliment, do you brush it off by pointing out where you are unworthy?

- How does that look? What do you say or do? What feelings are you trying to suppress by speaking to oppose the gift? Guilt? Obligation? Not wanting to appear needy?

- Are you able to genuinely feel comfortable receiving anything *without* immediately doing something in return? If someone gives you a gift, are you able to simply say, "Thank you"? Or do you feel the need to rush out and get something to pay her back?

- Do you carry a certain pride in being a giver? Do you sacrifice or deplete your own energy to be in service to others? How does this make you feel? What energetic benefit do you believe you gain from this one-sided exchange?

- How do you feel when you receive something without having "earned" it? If synchronicities happen to line up in your favor and something good happens in your life, how do you respond? To whom do you give the credit? God? Dumb luck? Fate? Are you quick to diminish your part in the blessing?

- Have you ever been punished or reprimanded in the past for doing well? For achieving highly? For surpassing others in your family, group, or tribe?

I invite you to sit with your discoveries for a little while, close your eyes, and let all the ideas and revelations gently bubble to the surface. Do not judge or resist them; simply allow them to appear as you and your higher awareness gently watch. Then consider the following:

- What do you notice as you observe these ideas? What emotions come up for you? Do you feel a sense of unworthiness, guilt, or shame? What, if any, memories are attached to them? Can you identify a belief about receiving that may operate as the origin of these feelings? What is the message for you?
- Can you be grateful for this message? Can you find benefit in it? How does this appreciation feel to you?

In order to alter energetic blocks, we must not resist them, since that causes greater distortion and only cements them more firmly in our consciousness. To dissolve them, we must break them apart with a higher frequency of energy. To break apart the obstacles to receiving, we must generate the energy of receiving, embody it, and focus our thinking and feeling mind on those obstacles. Just as in the old television commercial where an opera singer shatters a glass with the high frequency of her voice, we must shatter our distortions with a blast of sustained and focused vibration. The vibration we must use is the refined energy of *empowered* receiving.

EXERCISE
GENERATING THE POWER

Now that you are aware of your personal distortions related to receiving, I invite you to imagine what *genuine and empowered receiving* feels like. There is no right or wrong here, but the more precise you can be with your interpretation, the more powerful your outcome will be.

Please take a moment to close your eyes, take a couple of clearing breaths, relax, and gently say to yourself, "I am open and available to receive." Repeat this to yourself three times.

Once you have completed your repetitions, allow this

directive to engage itself within your energetic field. Notice what happens within your body. You may sense a shift, a buzz, or an opening. You may recognize a feeling of peace, well-being, or happiness. Simply observe without allowing your mind to interfere or justify. What vibrations or higher emotions do you notice? Allow this feeling to build within you for a couple of minutes.

As feelings and sensations start to become recognizable, acknowledge them by stating within, "Yes, I feel it. Yes, I sense it. There it is." Once you have consciously recognized the feeling, you must energetically "turn the volume up" on it. If the original feeling is at level 4, then use the power of focus and emotion to turn the volume up to level 6. What do you notice?

Hold that feeling for a few moments, then once again, using the power of focus and emotion, turn that feeling up, to level 8. What do you notice?

This energy that you are cultivating is your "giving" energy, but this is not done on the material plane; it is done energetically. *This* is the real meaning of: "In order to receive, you must first *give*."

Allow this feeling to soak into every cell of your being. Invite it to influence every space within your body and every aspect of your intuitive intelligence system. Encourage this energy to engage with the energetic field of your DNA and become one with your energy, so that there is no separation between you and it.

What does it feel like to have this level of energy available for you? What does it feel like to be given this without your having to say or do anything in return? What does it feel like to know that you are always connected and you always have access to this energy?

You may notice yourself becoming emotional. You may feel

an overwhelming desire to cry or shout. You may feel things in your body, like a pain in your neck or a tightness in your throat or chest. Do not resist these energies. The feelings that arise are energetic distortions that have held the blocks in place and are being released in order to let the new energy in. Allow whatever comes up to come up and move through you. Resist nothing.

This is where you get to give *again*. *Give* these energies up, give them away, surrender them to the power of your higher mind so they may be transformed and the energy that was once so tied up in holding them together is then released to serve you in your new choices.

Before you return to your present moment, take some time to become intimate with these higher vibrations of receiving. Let the sensations imprint themselves on your awareness, so that when you return to your day, all you will need to do when you require a boost of energy is remember them and re-create them within your energetic field.

As in all energetic exercises, I invite you to notice what you notice in your environment as you move back into your day. Pay attention to coincidences and synchronicities that align with the energy of receiving. Be aware of ideas, feelings, or impressions you may receive and that appear to come out of the blue. Acknowledge them whenever you notice them — write them down if you so desire; this will empower and reward your subconscious mind, encouraging it to continue doing the work. And it will inspire you to continue doing it to gain better and better results.

Eventually you will be able to generate this vibration without even thinking about it. It will have become a new habit, one that keeps you aligned with the energy of receiving at all times. Have fun with it, experiment with it, and see how its influence in your life makes your ability to receive seem almost miraculous.

CHAPTER 13

STEP 4:
NOTICING YOUR NOTICING

*The world is full of magic things, patiently waiting for our senses
to grow sharper.*

— W. B. YEATS

Becoming aware of the subtle processes of First Intelligence is
an adventure, and each of us has our own unique and specific
way of gathering and interpreting intuitive information. Because of
the work you have done up to this point, your expanded perceptions are now activated and more attuned to the subtle fields that
are the source of your intuitive solutions. With your conscious and
subconscious minds aligned in a common goal, your only job now is
to begin noticing what impulses, impressions, ideas, and imaginings
make their way to your expanded field of perception.

You may or may not have received a direct answer to your "ask"
during your meditation. If you did, that's great; but you must continue to stay alert because there is certain to be more information
forthcoming. And if you didn't get any direct information, that, too,
is fine, because intuitive intelligence is communicated in a wide variety of ways and most of them do *not* entail the direct or immediate
transmission of information.

I encourage you to be patient, trust yourself and the skills you are developing, and know that the information you are seeking will arrive. It is up to you to be present and available. If you are worried that you might be doing something wrong or missing out on things, then you will not be coherent enough or present enough to notice when the information is reaching you.

Our conscious mind, with its limited perceptiveness, does not have the vast scope of vision that our higher mind does. The higher mind holds solutions that are above and beyond what our myopic, programmed, and pragmatic ways of thought can generate, and the impressions we receive will never be the sorts of things that we normally would have considered through our regular, high-density thought processes. This is why we must never assume we know how or where the answer will find us, or what it will be, or what it will sound or look like when it shows up.

DID YOU CATCH THAT?

The information will find you, and you will know it is meant for you because it will grab your attention. It may be dramatic or subtle, but either way you will notice it. Your First Intelligence will use the path of least resistance the same way an electrical charge follows the path of least resistance. It will use the easiest way possible to gain your attention, based on who you are being at the moment. It serves you in the present moment, and it uses all the energies it has available *now* to provide you with direction. You do not need to go anywhere else, do anything different, or become someone else to use it.

The timing and reception of the requested information are based on our own internal timing and receptivity. How quickly we receive the information is always determined by our level of energy and our alignment with our goal. It also depends on our ability to handle or process the information based on our consciousness at the time.

Intuitive information can be perceived and received in a number of ways, and it is important to know the difference between them so that, if it doesn't show up in one particular way, you don't get angry, frustrated, or down on yourself or convince yourself that it isn't working right.

The modes of intuitive perception are active or passive, direct or symbolic, and synchronous or asynchronous.

Active Perception

Our intuition is said to be active when we can gather the information and guidance we need the moment we ask for it. Active intuition is present when we sit down to meditate and get an immediate answer, solution, or direction during the process of the meditation.

When I am working with a client or assisting with an investigation, active intuition is evident when I state my ask and the information is available without delay. This active form tends to become more predominant as you become more familiar with and proficient in your practice.

Passive Perception

This form of perception tends to work on a time delay, when the request for guidance is released into the field and the information is received hours, days, sometimes weeks later. The power of the information is no less profound, nor does our intelligence have to go anywhere to find it. It just takes us time to be in a receptive-enough state of mind to perceive it.

Information received while we are sleeping or dreaming could be considered passive perception, because while we sleep, the higher levels of brain function that are active during waking hours are diminished, allowing the intuitive information to connect through the resting mind.

Direct Perception

You experience direct perception when you receive information that is immediately understandable and the meaning of the impression is obvious to your conscious mind, requiring no interpretation. Impressions such as "Call Bob," "Look under the rug," or "Cake," as in my story about the shaman, or statements you overhear in a conversation or hear on the radio are directives you don't have to think about in order to follow their guidance. You may still not know why you are to follow the information, or how it applies to your immediate need, but there is no mistake about what it means to you.

Symbolic Perception

When the information perceived is more symbolic, metaphoric, or analogous in nature, you've received symbolic perception. You may notice certain impressions that do not immediately make sense but that contain symbolism holding a vast amount of information. You may notice certain animals appearing in your awareness, or see the same logo, plant, or piece of artwork again and again. You might have a recurring dream featuring a mythical creature, cartoon character, or angel. When you recognize these impressions, it is ultimately up to you to decide what they mean to you.

Symbolic perception of animals is prevalent in shamanic and Native American culture. The archetype of each animal is packed with information directly linked to the intention of the shaman or medicine man and can immediately provide guidance for the tribe or individual.

There is a deeper, hidden meaning in symbolic guidance. It will require a bit of effort on your part to interpret what the symbol means to you, but it can hold as much information as, or more than, direct perception. You can read books or go online to seek the general meaning behind certain symbols, but what it means and what resonates with you is up to you to decide. If the description feels right to you, then that is the message you are meant to hear.

Synchronous Perception

When information that we recognize comes to us in blocks or chunks, synchronous perception has occurred. This type of intuitive hit is known as a "download" and happens when the data is interpreted by the nervous system as a complete piece of information. In a single moment we recognize the entirety of a situation or circumstance; we recognize the big picture and we have a complete and solid understanding of what it is we are looking for.

Scientists like Einstein, Tesla, and even Steve Jobs all had profound synchronous experiences in which they could see the complete invention or solution in their mind's eye. All the information they needed to solve their problem or craft their new design was presented to them in one fell swoop.

Asynchronous Perception

This type of perception occurs when the data are not transmitted or received instantaneously or at a fixed rate but rather are perceived in little bits at a time, like our GPS guiding us to take step A, then step B, then step C, gently providing information as we need it and when it can best serve us. The inventors of the GPS knew that in order to begin a journey of a thousand miles, one has to pull out of the driveway first. Our intuition knows this fact as well.

This style of intuition often appears when a solution is detailed (by logical, material standards) and might require some space between steps to bring it to fruition. It is powerful in guiding us over great distances, and it helps us accomplish great things without overwhelming us with information.

No style of reception or perception is better or more powerful than any other. If your perception tends to be more passive than active, this does not mean you aren't as good at using your intuition as someone who perceives things more actively. Everyone experiences and benefits from all these perceptive styles at one time or another.

EXPANDED PERCEPTIONS AND THE SIX SENSES

First Intelligence uses the perceptions of every cell in the body to gather and interpret information from the environment, and as a result its language is predominantly driven by feeling and sensing. To be clear, this is not a language of "feeling" in an emotional way. It is a deeper, more subtle interpretation of the sensations triggered in the mind and body and of how they apply to your current need or situation.

As you develop your intuitive muscles, you will begin to relate to the environment differently than you may have before, and you will notice your perception expanding in ways that go beyond your previous understandings and physical limitations. The world is not changing, but your ability to sense things within that framework is.

The following are the most common forms of intuitive perception.

What You Know: Claircognizance, or Clear Knowing

The ability to perceive intuitive information via inner knowing or direct physical sensation, this intuitive skill lets you determine that something is true or accurate without any supporting knowledge or rational explanation. Because claircognizance is not sourced in a specific physical sense organ, it may be harder to identify and develop. But because the knowledge or information is direct and is experienced powerfully, it is less likely to be misinterpreted or questioned by the logical mind. The knowledge often appears as a complete picture or understanding of a person, situation, or circumstance that is accurate and detailed without any previous experience or exposure to it.

This type of information most commonly comes in active, synchronous, and direct modalities.

Statements linked to claircognizance: "I just knew I was going to get that job." "I just knew I shouldn't drive to work today."

While "clear knowing" is usually considered an intuitive superpower, the expanded perceptions of the other five senses seem to be more commonly developed, and through those we gain the most consistent and useful information.

The Big Five

We are all, of course, aware of the external ability to see, taste, touch, smell, and hear as we interact with the physical world around us. But we constantly use the inner abilities of our senses as well. We have all experienced inner vision when having a dream, used our inner sense of taste and smell when fantasizing about a great meal, used inner hearing when recalling the voice of a loved one, and used inner feeling when remembering any sort of intense experience. We use our spiritual senses all the time, so the ability to consciously use them as intuitive tools is an easy transition to make.

It is important to be aware of how your sense of expanded intuitive perception is going to manifest itself, both on the outer screen of your reality and on the inner one. As you make it a point to notice what you notice, it's important to understand how your focused intention has altered your ability to perceive.

What You See: Clairvoyance, or Clear Seeing

The ability to perceive intuitive information through the sense of sight, or vision, is often strongest in someone who learns or remembers best through visual means. It manifests through mental imagery, inner photo slide shows, or mini–mind movies. If you have this ability, you can clearly visualize a solution or see the big picture.

Clairvoyance is active in the following ways:

- You may notice certain colors, fields of vibration, or waves of heat around someone who is ill, in a bad mood, or just plain awful to be around. Conversely, you may receive different visual impressions if the person is beneficial to your well-being or success.

- Your attention may be drawn to a billboard on the freeway or a headline in a newspaper that holds a particular word or message pertaining to your need.

- You may notice a brand name or logo in the market or on someone's T-shirt that inspires you to make a call or pursue an idea.

- You may notice seeing the same thing over and over again wherever you go, such as numbers, colors, balloons, clowns, or grasshoppers, each of which can have a symbolic meaning that addresses your request for guidance.

- You may see a vision of an invention, idea, or creative endeavor completely formed in your mind's eye while meditating, dreaming, or napping.

Statements connected to clairvoyance: "I just didn't like the look of him." "I could see how it would all work out."

What You Hear: Clairaudience, or Clear Hearing

The ability to perceive intuitive information through the sense of sound, or hearing, is often strongest in someone who learns or remembers best by listening. Such a person will then remember the words or voice to recall the teaching. People with strong musical tendencies often have this highly developed intuitive tool.

Clairaudience is active in the following ways:

- You may recognize music, words, sentences, or thoughts that hold information and guidance related to your current need. Pay attention to the sounds, noises, vibrations, and tones you notice both in the external environment and within your own inner hearing.

- The audient impressions may sound like your everyday thoughts, or you may sometimes interpret them as coming from behind or beside you. These impressions are inaudible to normal hearing and will not be perceived by others.

- Do the particular words of a song you hear on the radio seem to resonate with you in a powerful way, or do you wake up with a song in your head that holds a pertinent or meaningful message?

- Do parts of other people's conversations frequently contain particular words that seem meaningful in relation to your current need?

- Is there a buzzing or a ringing in your ears that seems to come and go, or that seems more active during certain activities? When you notice it, take a moment to stop, acknowledge it, and ask what the message is.

Inner statements connected to clairaudience: "That just doesn't sound right." "It was like music to my ears."

What You Feel: Clairsentience, or Clear Feeling

The ability to perceive intuitive information through the sense of touch, vibration, or feeling is often strongest in people who tend to focus on how things feel, either physically or emotionally. People who learn kinesthetically — that is, by doing — commonly excel at this level of intuitive intelligence. This is often the intelligence most strongly linked to feminine intuition, because many women tend to have heightened body awareness due to their monthly cycles.

Psychometry, the ability to gather intuitive information by touching an object, such as a piece of jewelry, clothing, or even a photograph, is an expanded form of clairsentience.

Strong feelings of empathy, engagement, and compassion are common with this sense. This level of perception links you to information in the environment that might be linked to other people's emotions, to physical or mental conditions, or to unseen circumstances such as chemical, electrical, or mechanical influences that may or may not be beneficial to you.

Clairsentience can be recognized in the following ways:

- Pay attention to what you notice through your feeling nature; this may be through physical touch or internal emotional touch.

- Pay attention to what you feel within your body when greeting someone for the first time. Is there a temperature shift within you when you shake hands? Does your head hurt? Do you feel sad or agitated? These may be signs that meeting this person is not in your best interests and that you should proceed with caution.

- Do you notice a sense of lightness, expansion, or well-being in your body when engaging with a certain person or experience? Does your heart open? Do you notice a sense of enthusiasm? These may be signs that this person or experience is beneficial for you or can assist you in fulfilling your current need.

- Do you notice a certain feeling within your body when holding, touching, or tasting a certain food or medicine? These impressions may be guiding you to notice whether it is beneficial for you.

- What do you notice when stepping into a particular room or environment? What is your body saying to you? These are indications of the level of supportive or beneficial energies within the environment.

Inner statements connected to clairsentience: "It just doesn't feel right to me." "That guy is a pain in my ass."

What You Smell: Clairalience, or Clear Smelling

This is the ability to perceive intuitive information through the sense of smell. Never underestimate the power of smell as a tool for gaining intuitive information. The sense of smell is ten thousand times more powerful than the others because the olfactory nerves go directly into our limbic brain without having to travel through the nervous system. Data reveal that people who are deaf, blind, or both have highly tuned olfactory systems and can instantly recognize people, places, and things by smell alone.

Clairalience is active in the following ways:

- Do you notice an odor or an aroma when you ask for guidance in your meditations? A putrid or bitter smell might indicate an unwise decision, while the smell of cookies, roses, or forest air might indicate a wise choice.

- Is there a smell or aroma that catches your attention seemingly from out of the blue while you are going about your daily activities? It might be the smell of your mother's perfume, your grandfather's cigar, or the smell of an old leather chair. What memory does this aroma trigger, and how can it guide you in your current situation?

- Do you notice a sense of anxiety or well-being when you meet or spend time with a certain person? While you may not be conscious of it, your sense of smell may be picking up hormones secreted by the other person that may indicate anxiety, anger, or frustration. Conversely, you may perceive the chemicals of peace, happiness, and ease, which instantly affect your field and your experience of well-being.

Inner statements connected to clairalience: "That deal really stinks." "Smells rosy to me."

What You Taste: Clairgustance, or Clear Tasting

The ability to perceive intuitive information through the sense of taste is rare. It allows us to interpret the essence of a person, situation, or circumstance via the perception of tastes or sensations in the mouth. This sense can be perceived in dramatic and obvious ways, such as experiencing the taste of blood, sugar, cigarettes, medicine, food, or chemicals while nothing is present in the mouth.

Clairgustance is active in the following ways:

- Do you notice any sort of taste or mouth sensation when introduced to someone during an important meeting? This may also manifest itself as mouth watering or mouth dryness. If a taste or sensation is noticeable, what does it mean to you?

- Do you notice that your sense of taste is "off" or disrupted when eating something that wouldn't normally bother you? Does your favorite food suddenly taste bitter, or is something hard to swallow? This could signal something out of alignment within your body, or it could be a response to something recognized within the environment. What could your mouth be trying to communicate to you?

Inner statements connected to clairgustance: "That leaves a bad taste in my mouth." "I find what he is saying hard to swallow."

Your nervous system is constantly interpreting information that will let you know if a person or situation is aligned with your highest good. You may need to do some deeper interpretation to define the message, but if you noticed it and you notice that you noticed it, use it.

ACKNOWLEDGE WHAT YOU NOTICE

Whenever you notice an intuitive hit or impression, or recognize a coincidence or synchronicity, it is important to immediately say to yourself, "Yes, I see it. Yes, I notice it. Yes, I have recognized the information. Thank you." This is an instance of the conscious mind linking with and strengthening its connection with the subconscious mind, which facilitates the integration, communication, and effectiveness of both.

This simple step strengthens and rewards your subconscious mind, like giving a treat to a pet who performs a task properly. The elevated feeling of gratitude and acknowledgment is like an electrical cookie that rewards the subconscious for properly performing a task. This makes the subconscious mind more prone to continue the good behavior. And because this level of mind is compulsive, it will feel compelled to continue to provide you with the information you seek. The act becomes automatic, ingrained, and shifts from something you need to focus and concentrate on, to something that is natural and automatic.

At this point it is not up to you to take action; that will come next. You need only signal the subconscious mind that it has done its job well and that you are grateful.

WRITE IT DOWN

Often your observations will be profound enough that you'll remember the impression without effort, but I encourage you to write down everything you notice. The simple act of putting these impressions down on paper begins an alchemical process of making the ideas and impressions real — the physical action and material result of putting the information provided by your intuition on a piece of paper is the first stage of turning energy into matter.

If your perceptions are symbolic, writing them down gives you the opportunity to begin any interpretation, if necessary. If you find yourself working with a symbolic direction, it can be beneficial to draw it and then, in a quiet, coherent state, ask your intuition, "What does this symbol mean for me?" Then, without editing, analyzing, or rationalizing it, write down what you hear, feel, and notice. This relaxed writing will often hold the answer hidden in the symbolic message.

We want our First Intelligence to provide us with expanded and innovative information, so we should expect it to be an idea we have never considered before, a path to take that we would not normally venture down, or a plan of action that we would not normally pursue. Our observations should please, inspire, and delight us. They can and often do tickle our funny bone, activate our sense of joy, and bring a feeling of wonder and lightness to our daily experience. You will know you are on the right track when the things you perceive align with the answer or result you seek and are moving you forward.

If you receive impressions that tell you to go back and do something over again, or to return to an old pattern of behavior, you can bet with 100 percent certainty that your lower mind has done some sneaky maneuvering, and you have some energetic housekeeping to do.

Make it a part of your daily routine to expect the unexpected and to be completely willing to experience the unknown. This is the widest doorway you can provide for your intuition to step through. Then it will be up to you to be courageous and flexible enough to follow the direction and take some important and empowered action.

GETTING TO KNOW THE SOUND OF YOU

In learning to become intimate with your own intuitive language, solitude matters. Unfortunately, we live in a society of endless mental, social, physical, and emotional stimulation with an ever-quickening media and entertainment cycle and a culture that thrives on "doing" instead of "being." All this external noise constantly agitates our inner environment, making it virtually impossible to hear the still, quiet voice of our inner knowing.

It is no accident that the greatest teachers of transcendent wisdom knew the inherent value of and power in solitary reflection and made it a part of their practice to travel alone, often into the wilderness to gain favor with and communicate with divine intelligence.

The ancient mystics and medicine men all knew that the path that leads us deeply within must first be cleared of any psychic debris before real communication with divine wisdom can occur. In order for us as modern mystics to access the same realm of intelligence, we too must journey to our own inner wilderness to see what we discover there and what, if anything, it might have to tell us.

NAME YOUR TUNE

Austrian composer Gustav Mahler once said, "A symphony must be like the world. It must contain everything." Well, I am no composer, but I do enjoy beautiful music, and it is my humble opinion that if a symphony contained everything, all it would produce would be noise.

Unfortunately, noise is what we have all around us in our modern world, and our senses both inner and outer are subjected to a constant cacophony of energetic irritants. Imagine that everyone in the world today is a musical instrument playing in a symphony orchestra, and that they have all been loosed in the streets to play their tunes. We are all familiar with how an orchestra sounds when it is warming up for a performance; "a joyful noise" would not be an appropriate description of the discordant deluge on our senses.

All the people we know intimately and casually, personally and professionally, play their instruments in this world orchestra, too, and their vibrations influence us every moment we are in their company. Our families create a specific vibration, people from our places of employment create another unique vibration, and people from our community, our country, and the world create still others.

These vibrations are commonly known as the group mind, or collective consciousness, and are cultivated by the ideas, beliefs, laws, rules, dogmas, attitudes, emotions, and past history of each of the collaborators. The consciousness of each group morphs and shifts as old players leave and new players arrive on the stage, with each individual contributing to the dynamic of the whole and ultimately determining the shape of the reality in that environment. If we are not aware of our own inner vibrations, separately from the dictates of the whole, then the group mind can easily influence us and it becomes virtually impossible to discern the sound of our own inner wisdom through the din.

With all the noise around us, we wouldn't know the sound of our own music if our lives depended on it. And sometimes it does.

QUIETING THE CHATTER

Psychologists tell us that we mirror and mimic people's ideas and behaviors without even noticing. Groups will follow the opinions of the most charismatic, dare I say loudest and most consistent, voice in the room regardless of whether what that person is saying is true, valid, or wise. This is not hard to recognize when the people speaking the loudest, yet making the least sense, are often the most successful at gaining an audience. Just look at media, advertising, entertainment, politics, and television news, and you will see how this all plays out. The loudest drum determines the rhythm of the entire performance.

With all this external noise it is difficult to know what is the truth or how to recognize which path is truly the right one to follow. It can be overwhelming, and when confusion sets in, many people become paralyzed and make no decisions at all. So we ask everyone else for their opinions, or we go to a therapist or see another psychic, and still we do not feel confident that we can recognize the truth. At this point it becomes easier to simply fall in with everyone else, becoming part the group mind, regardless of how painful, unfulfilling, and inauthentic it may be to do so.

There is no parent, therapist, expert, or psychic who has a more direct link to what is true for you than you do. Your intuitive intelligence is the only life adviser you will ever need, and if anyone should ever tell you to disregard your own inner wisdom, reevaluate your connection with him or her.

Do you even know who you really are outside of your relationship or job or title? When was the last time you clearly heard the voice of your true self, away from the kids pounding on the door, your husband asking where his socks are, the sound of the TV, and the pull of your cell phone? How many excuses do you make that prevent you from engaging in this ultimate tool of evolution and survival?

Solitude allows us to reengage with the frequencies of our inner world and gives us time and space to recognize who we are within ourselves as conscious beings. This understanding will be crucial as you move forward in your intuitive practice, because once you become intimate with how you feel within yourself, away from the influences of friends, family, and the world at large, never again will you be confused or paralyzed by the avalanche of external opinion. And never again will your ability to betray yourself be as powerful as it once was. Your soul simply will not allow it.

When you become intimate with and learn to recognize your inner sound, you will know in a heartbeat when you are receiving information or data aligned with your highest good — and you will know just as clearly when you are being fed a line of crap. Solitude allows you to fine-tune the greatest lie detector and truth serum ever created, the one that is part of your own biology.

EXERCISE
RECOGNIZING YOUR FIELD

Create some time *at least* once a week (but really a *daily* practice is recommended) to take a walk alone in nature without a cell phone, iPod, or other distraction. No kidding here. Leave your technology at home or in the car, and see what you notice about your own inner field of energy. Taking your dog with you should not be considered a distraction; taking your kids is.

Walks in nature are fabulous opportunities to do some great intuitive discovery, but before you begin using this time to do intuitive "work," allow yourself the time to simply be in this space without making it about anything other than getting a sense of the feel of your inner world.

During the first few minutes of your walk, simply observe how you feel within the environment. Smell the smells, fill your lungs with the clean air, feel the crunch of earth beneath your feet, notice the colors and the temperature, and engage all your senses. Become one with the environment, and make it your intention to regulate and return your body to the balanced rhythms of nature.

With continued exposure to this environment, you will notice that the vibration of your body gains more depth or resonance; you may notice a hum, a buzz, or a low-grade tingle. You may feel your heart and head expand or a general sense of well-being flowing through your system. Pay attention to how this energy shifts, accelerates, or becomes amplified in tone or feeling. It is your energetic field discharging all the interference and beginning to regain its natural coherence.

If you go away on vacation and find that it takes you a while to unwind and enjoy it, this is a sign that your body is severely depleted of coherent energy and that you need to increase your daily intake of Mother Nature. If it has been a while since you were surrounded by anything that could be considered natural, then it may take a while to let go of the vibrations and frequencies of industrialized life. Be patient. Eventually your body will remember what living energy feels like and begin soaking it up like a sponge.

Doing this work regularly will help you recalibrate and recognize your energetic base level — that is, you will be able to identify who you are as a vibration or frequency without any external influences on your field. With practice these subtle vibrations will become easier to recognize, and ultimately you will be able to amplify them as your skills increase.

Letting Go of Your Opinions

Notice as much of the world around you as you can, without any interpretation or judgment. If you see a particularly ugly bug, don't have any inner conversation about it; just observe it and notice your inner environment as you do. If you spot a gorgeous animal or bird, simply watch it doing its thing. Don't form an opinion about its beauty, but notice what, if anything, happens within you. Expand this practice to include people you may notice on your walk; but again, simply observe them and pay attention to how your body feels when they get closer to you or move farther away, all without judgment or inner commentary.

You may be surprised to see how busy your mind is with inner chatter, and how vigilant it is about categorizing, commenting on, and criticizing what it experiences. When our mind is busy with commentary, it misses out on the subtle cues intuition provides, which may make the difference between achieving our highest good and being too distracted to notice the beneficial information that is being presented to us.

Fixed opinions, good or bad, put the brakes on intuitive perception and skew your ability to recognize accurate information. Regardless of the severity of a crime scene, the urgency to find a child, or the frustration of the mess someone has created in his life, any opinion I have about good or bad, right or wrong, victim or perpetrator, must be completely and honestly released before I begin my intuitive work. If my request for information is clouded by my judgments, this will deeply affect the quality of information I perceive and I will be of little or no service to anyone.

When you can recognize your vibration without the influence of an opinion attached to it, you will know that your request for intuitive information will not be influenced by wishful thinking or limitation. You will know how it feels when your field is clear before you engage with it.

The stakes in your own situation may be very high — you may be dealing with a severe illness, a grave financial situation, or some sort of life-altering decision. But if you hold an opinion about it, you are judging the whole of it, even the solution. To have an opinion about anything is to have an opinion about everything.

Notice the thoughts or feelings that come up, positive or negative, and do not resist them. Rather, gracefully engage them and ask what message of wisdom or healing they hold. This practice develops your ability to completely engage with an environment and allow the vibratory impressions to influence your field while, at the same time, you maintain a neutral mental position or opinion. This skill can assist you in gathering appropriate energetic information when meeting people for the first time, when considering whether a place to live or to work is appropriate, and even when determining if a food or medicine is beneficial for you.

CHAPTER 14

STEP 5:
INTERPRETATION

No one saves us but ourselves. No one can and no one may. We ourselves must walk the path. Buddhas only show the way.

— BUDDHA

Interpretation is a small but rich and essential part of your intuitive work, and it can be great fun discovering the power of meaningful messages held within a seemingly inert piece of information. This is the part of the work where you get to play mystical detective in order to get to the root of an answer, and where you will be amazed at the level of humor and wit our intuition possesses when it presents us with life-changing information hidden in a simple symbol.

It is important to learn to trust your ability to properly discern the messages conveyed in the guidance you receive — this is an aspect of precision. This part of the work tends to cause some people a bit of distress because they fear not doing it right. But once folks get the hang of it, it becomes the part they most look forward to and have the most fun with.

I invite you to do this part of the work with a sense of joy and a lightness of heart. Release your serious, grown-up self and allow your inner child to come out and play — you know, the one who could see bunnies and dragons in the clouds and who made super-hero capes out of beach towels.

This youthful part of you is relentlessly honest. Even if the reason you are doing the intuitive inquiry is deeply serious, it will be this lighthearted spirit that activates the creativity of your intuitive mind and finds the meaning in the messages. If you can agree to invite this side of yourself to participate in the process, you will be rewarded by insight and clarity that your grown-up self could never hope to muster.

KEEP YOUR EYES ON YOUR OWN WORK

I encourage you to do your *own* interpretation and not to ask others to interpret your messages, perceptions, or dreams for you. This is important for a number of reasons. To ask other people for their opinions or interpretations does not empower you, nor does it assist you in developing confidence in your practice. Asking other people for interpretation is also a signal to your subconscious mind that you don't believe you have what it takes to get it right.

Most people ask for other people's opinions when they are trying to avoid getting something wrong. Remember, while developing our intuitive proficiency, we need to become comfortable with making mistakes. Ironically, it is asking for other people's interpretations of our intuitive perceptions that ultimately will cause us to err. Other people's interpretations are filtered through their belief systems, attitudes, expectations, and emotions, so to bring your intuitive information to someone and ask them what they think it means will only further your confusion.

If I see a dog in one of my intuitive sessions, the guidance I perceive in it may be radically different from what others perceive as a result of their beliefs and attitudes about dogs. Your intuitive direction is crafted specifically to suit your unique, personal energetic system, and no one else can or should offer interpretations to serve you.

Many therapists spend years learning how to interpret dreams, and there are countless books on the market that guide readers to make decisions based on symbols as they are interpreted by the author. Feel free to use these resources as guides, but do not take the information in them as the word of law simply because it is written in a book or someone has a diploma on the wall. There is no standard, one-size-fits-all answer that will precisely direct every person as specifically as the intuitive mind of the individual himself.

However, if you are *really* struggling to find an answer (which from my experience is rare) and you feel you must ask for help, then share your vision or symbol with someone you trust, someone you feel has a certain level of spiritual maturity. Ask her what it would mean to *her* if *she* had received it in a directive meant to assist *her*. Don't ask what she thinks it means for *you*. Then you can decide if that interpretation holds any meaning for you and use it accordingly. But chances are, it won't, and you will have wasted your time and energy looking for the answers that you already have within yourself.

Part of becoming proficient at using your intuition is learning to trust your own interpretations and to recognize how they apply directly to you. I highly recommend you do your own work. You will be amazed at how brilliant you are.

A PICTURE HOLDS A THOUSAND WORDS

There are two parts to the interpretation process: clarification and interpretation. Clarifying what you perceived gives you the opportunity to "get clear" about it and to interpret it more accurately.

To clarify your information, ask, "What did I notice? What stood out for me? What did I see? Hear? Recognize? Feel moved by? Did it have a direct meaning for me, and if so what was it? If it wasn't direct, but I still noticed it, can I determine that there is a symbolic meaning here somewhere?"

If it is symbolic, what was the symbol? What did it look like? How many were there? Were there colors that stood out? Or sounds? Or feelings? Is it a number? What were the surroundings? Is it a commercial logo or brand of some kind? Write down as many of the details of what you saw as you can remember, but without interpreting them. You can even draw them if you like. Once you have recorded them, and while still maintaining your relaxed sense of peace and play, you can move on to the second step, interpretation.

Now you get to ask questions that will assist you in finding the deeper meaning of the symbol. Does it remind you of anyone you know or anything you have experienced before? Does a phrase or group of words come to mind when you think of it? How do you feel when you think of it? Does the symbol have a specific meaning or generate any emotion for you? If so what is it?

Allow yourself to ask as many questions along these lines as you can come up with. Allow them to flow in a relaxed way. There are no wrong questions to ask. Your goal at this moment is to be a kind and loving investigator whose only desire is to find clarity. Write the questions down as you ask them of yourself, and then go directly to writing down the answers without editing, analyzing, or judging them. Write down the *first* thing that comes to mind when you ask the question.

If an answer does not appear within five seconds, then move on to the next question. To wait any longer than that gives the thinking mind time to click into gear, and at this point in the process thinking is a no-no. Once you have asked and answered what you feel is the appropriate number of questions, take a few moments to review what you have written down. Do you notice words that are repeated over and over? Circle them. Do those words hold meaning for you? If so, what is that meaning?

What did you discover about the meaning within those symbols? Does it resonate with you in a solid way? It doesn't have to make sense at this point, and you don't need to know why this symbol appeared or where it is meant to lead you. Just feel your connection with it.

Does your interpretation offer you an answer or direction to the question posed in your "ask"? If so, can you take immediate action? If not, could you ask more questions to find deeper clarity? If the answer is still no, can you still take action on it without knowing the how or why of where it will lead you?

Interpreting symbols is a highly personal process. There are no hard-and-fast rules about what they mean. The following stories are examples of how to decipher the subtle yet deeply intricate messages found in symbolism.

KAELA

I was feeling really stuck. In one morning meditation, and in a frustrated way, I must admit, I asked my intuition for a sign, for help, for something to show me that I was on the right track.

Later that day, as I was driving home after running errands, the idea of the book Three Feet from Gold *flashed into my head.[1] It had been published several years earlier, and although I had never read it I had heard of it and knew its message: many people give up on their dreams or desires right before reaching the vein of success hidden in the unseen potential around them. They quit "three feet from gold."*

I didn't feel compelled to rush out and buy the book, but I noticed that I had noticed it and continued on home.

When I did get home, I noticed a green scarab-type beetle on my porch, right in front of my door. It was stuck on its back and was struggling to right itself. I picked up a stick and gently offered it to the beetle, who immediately climbed on board, flipped itself right side up, and flew away in a flashy buzz.

I knew that this type of beetle had many spiritual meanings in ancient cultures, so I looked it up online. I discovered that a green beetle was considered a symbol of wealth and prosperity, rebirth and renewal, which of course were the things I was currently frustrated with.

I didn't put the two impressions together until my next meditation, when I once again asked for clarity and direction and the images of the book and the beetle flashed into my mind. In that moment the message became clear, and both symbols began to resonate deeply within me. The message was: "Keep up your practice; do not give up. You may feel stuck and frustrated right now, but you are on the right track. You are close; success is near. Soon you will fly."

This was precisely the message I needed to hear: that I wasn't broken or going about creating my dream life in the wrong way. It empowered me to shift out of my anxiety and back into flow and gratitude.

JAKE

I was trying to decide whether I should invest with a company that a friend had brought to my attention. I had heard mixed reports about it and wasn't sure who I should trust.

I did my intuitive workout to see if I could be guided in the proper direction. I sat for a few minutes and noticed nothing. It was hard to become coherent at first, because I really wanted to receive the right information. I had been saving my money for a long time and I didn't want to make a huge mistake.

Then, just before I was about to quit, I heard the sound swoosh. It wasn't a buzz or whirrrr or snap. It was swoosh. I *sat for a few more minutes, hoping that the sound wouldn't be all I got out of the session, that I would hear a voice guiding me in one way or another.*

It doesn't always work that way, so I got up from my workout and noticed what I noticed. The only thing I recalled was swoosh.

So I did my interpretation. Swoosh. *What does that mean to me? The words and images I got were:* speed, air, light, fast, *and the logo that Nike uses, the swoosh. All those things made me feel active, alive, gave me the impression of moving forward.*

Then I asked the question "What does Nike mean to me?" and I remembered their tagline, "Just do it."

I laughed! "Oh, please. Yeah, right!" I thought. "It can't be that simple!" But I really wanted to learn how to trust this intuition thing, so even though I was nervous about it, I called my friend later that afternoon and told him I was in.

I didn't trust the swoosh *100 percent, though, and invested only half my savings — which turned out to be fine anyway, because the company ended up doing really well.*

Learning to completely trust the process and put my faith in something as obscure as a word like swoosh *will take some practice. To be honest, I don't know if it will ever be easy. But I do know that, at least this time, it worked out in my favor.*

LIVING SYMBOLICALLY

Learning to interpret symbols will change how you perceive and respond to meaning in every aspect of your life. It will become something you use everywhere, not only in moments of intuitive practice. Because of the deep and profound information found in the simplest of things, you will start to recognize messages hidden in seemingly mundane and random occurrences.

Symbolic sight invites you to step out of the limited, myopic way of seeing life and leads you into an often-mystical conversation with nature and the world around you. It empowers you to see the meaning in everything that has ever happened to you, both good and bad, and provides you with the clarity necessary to put those situations in their rightful place as builders of the path to your chosen destiny.

CHAPTER 15

STEP 6:
TAKING INSPIRED ACTION

It had long since come to my attention that people of accomplishment rarely sat back and let things happen to them. They went out and happened to things.

— LEONARDO DA VINCI

Taking action seems as if it might be the most straightforward part of this intuitive adventure, but just as in every other aspect of your practice, there is a level of precision and understanding necessary to make it as valuable a process as possible. And just as in every other facet we have focused on so far, there is a physical aspect to taking action and a spiritual aspect to taking action.

It is important to realize that taking action is not always going to be limited to the things you do in the physical world. We are often guided to take even greater action in our inner world before any direction for external action is forthcoming.

INNER ACTION

Before you take any major action on the physical plane, ask yourself, "What am I willing to let go of within myself in order to create my desired outcome? What beliefs, attitudes, or emotions are prevent-ing me from creating success?"

The actions you take to change your *consciousness* will be the most powerful agents for healing, success, empowerment, or love that you can use. Remember, the point of our intuitive work is *not* to try to force the outside world to be different than it is but to change our inner levels of mind, awareness, and perception so that the shifts we make within us are reflected on the outward screen of our reality.

Consciousness creates. Personality doesn't. Spirit and the attri-butes of the higher mind are creative forces. Matter is a physical out-come. We must take great action on the inside to give what we do on the outside real power. Otherwise it amounts to nothing more than moving a bunch of bricks around the yard and then putting them back in the same position, hoping that you end up with something different than before.

Many people are disappointed when they ask their intuition, "What action do I take now?" and the answer they receive is "For-give." They think they are doing it wrong, or that their guidance system isn't working right, or that somehow they have gotten their signals crossed. But this is not the case.

In fact, such a statement is a direction to embody a higher vibra-tion of mind and heart. Forgiveness and similar acts are spiritual in nature and so have the power to alter or shift lower-frequency vibra-tions that take shape physically — such as poor health, financial frustration, lack of relationship, or virtually anything else deemed to be negative in the physical world. While this may be a deep under-standing in the realm of the higher mind, it can be a tough pill to swallow for the lower mind and the wounded ego.

This part of the work tends to elicit the most resistance from people, because they don't understand that creating a new destiny is an inside job, and that the majority of the work required to create a new outcome is not done on the physical level.

Certainly there will be many times when an intuitive direction will guide you to *do* something, like make a phone call, stop eating a certain food, set up a new daily routine, move to a new city, or design a new product. But doing different things on the material plane *as an initial action* will not have the biggest effect on your outcome.

Our intuition will often guide us to relax, allow, let go, laugh, or resist nothing, *first*. Then it will instruct us that the time is right to leave a job, write a book, start a new company, or go on that date.

NOTHING IS FREE

As I mentioned earlier, in order to create the outcome you desire you must be willing to actively let go of certain aspects of yourself that have gotten you to this moment. If you are to receive the benefits of a new life situation, there must be space within your consciousness where those benefits can land. Life cannot add anything to a cup that is already full. Creating new realities requires you to alter, change, or completely give up the thoughts, beliefs, emotions, and attitudes that you have been using in your life so far.

There have been countless times in workshops and coaching sessions when people have asked me how they can use their intuition to assist them in finding their perfect relationship partner. When this query comes up, I respond by asking two sets of questions: First I ask the individual to tell me what kind of person he is seeking and then to list the attributes of who he believes himself to be.

This is a generalization, but most often the ideal partner is described as attractive, kind, funny, financially secure, sensitive to others, self-confident, emotionally and physically healthy, self-aware, drama-free, spiritual, and so on. For most people, generating a list of ways for someone *else* to be is fun and easy. But the second set of questions I ask isn't always as easy for them to answer: What are you willing to give up or let go of? What price are you willing to pay to create that ideal partnership?"

The questions often surprise people, because up until now they have not considered the fact that in order to have, do, or be something other than what they are having, doing, or being right now, they must be someone other than they have been. It can work no other way. Remember, this is an *energetic* question, not a physical one.

The type of person they just described is going to have specific parameters about who *they* are looking for, the type of person *they* want to have in *their* life. A person like this will not want to be with someone who is petty, childish, demanding, neurotic, insecure, lazy, or selfish. Energies of a similar nature are attracted to one another; those of opposite polarities repel. If you want a specific sort of person as a partner, you will have to resonate with them energetically.

The same costs would apply if you wanted to become a millionaire. Wealth and success come to a person who continually exhibits thoughts, emotions, mind-sets, and beliefs that align with the principles of abundance. Wealth will not partner with you if you hold on to your fear, lack, unworthiness, and insecurity.

Health will not partner with you if you hold on to your anger, resentment, bitterness, or hostility. Success will not partner with you if you hold on to your sense of limitation, shame, or fear. There are no exceptions to this principle of attraction and repulsion. You will have to be deeply honest about what parts of yourself are preventing you from achieving your goal. You will also need to be committed to immediately and permanently letting go of those aspects. The bottom line is, you must be willing to pay the energetic price.

You can begin this inner action plan immediately by asking your intuitive self, "What am I willing to let go of within myself to create my desired outcome? What beliefs, attitudes, or emotions are standing in my way?" And then notice what you notice.

When you become aware of these negative attributes, acknowledge them, appreciate them for being a part of you, thank them for being of service to you, and release them to the power of your higher mind (your superconsciousness) to be returned to the field of all possibility.

MEDITATION FOR LETTING GO

Take a few moments to first generate your foundation of peace and coherence. Remember that all our intuitive work must begin within the elevated vibratory field of the higher mind. When you feel you have settled into a feeling of well-being, state silently or aloud, "I thank my intuitive mind for revealing this block to me. I acknowledge and appreciate that (the attribute) has been brought to my attention. Thank you, (attribute), for being a part of me and for serving me for so long, but I choose to release you at this time. It is with gratitude and appreciation that I surrender you to the power of my higher mind. I ask that divine wisdom take this obstacle from me and return it to the field of all possibility, so there is room within my mind, body, and spirit to receive the abundant possibility of my greatest desire through peace and right action. Thank you."

Make this meditation a part of your daily intuitive practice. You will know that it is working to make space within you when you feel a greater sense of ease, peace, lightness, and well-being. This meditation offers you a way to take action on the inner planes by breaking down the barriers that cloud your perception. It will begin to free up the energy your mind and body need in order to take action in the material world.

OUTER ACTION

The way you go about taking an outer action is just as important as the way you find the direction in the first place. Jumping into any action with a sense of fear and insecurity will negate the positive work you have done on the inner realms. It is important to move forward with any action you might take from a state of calm appreciation, all the while maintaining your vision and energy in the peaceful expectation of your completed goal.

As the amplitude and power of your coherence grow, and as coherence becomes your natural state of being, you will find yourself receiving direction that grows more precise and elegant. And you will have less and less uncertainty when following its direction. It does require a bit of practice to develop the confidence to trust information you perceive. But eventually you will learn to distinguish between the bits of information that are meant to guide you to your highest good and the ones that are simply remnants of your old way of thinking, which can be gently left at the side of the road.

Regardless of how coherent you become, or how well you generate a great ask, recognize your style, or notice what you notice, at the end of the day none of it will do you one whit of good unless you follow the directions you receive. This part of the process really isn't complicated. When you notice an intuitive direction, follow it. Respond to it. Act on it.

If the response to your question "What action do I take first?" leaves you with the impression that you must connect with a certain person, connect with that person. If you get the impression that you must visit another city, start planning a trip that will get you there. If you receive a vision or idea for a new invention, book, or idea, start putting your ideas down on paper. Draw them or write them out as completely as possible without allowing interference from your lower mind. If you hear, "Turn left," for Pete's sake, turn left!

When we allow the rationalization of the logical, thinking mind to sneak in, which many of us know as "analysis paralysis," we don't move, we don't take action, and we don't change our lives. The fear of doing it wrong has stepped in to try to figure out the most certain way to avoid making a mistake, and the discomfort we feel in those moments is an indication that we have turned away from the calm power of our deepest inner wisdom.

Take the action. Make the call. Send the email with a feeling of grace, ease, and a certain peace, knowing that you are taking a step forward in a new direction. At this moment, chances are pretty good that you have no idea where it is going to lead you, nor do you know precisely how it will look when you get there. But you know what you know, and you also know that maybe, for the first time ever, you are following your heart.

Take the action, then release it. Give it some time to take shape and see what happens. You may not always get immediate results from your actions, especially if they require a follow-up action from someone else. You may not always get positive feedback. You may not always get any result at all. This is normal. Do not become discouraged by this; do not think that because your guidance and the action you took in response did not result in a huge success you have failed. You have *not*, by any stretch of the imagination, failed. Remember: who you are becoming through the process of taking action is of greater importance here!

Taking action requires you to develop courage and accept responsibility for the direction of your life. Taking action requires you to stop playing small, and it will prove to you time and time again that this action stuff isn't so scary, even if it doesn't turn out precisely the way you expect it to. Taking action teaches you to develop trust in your own choices and to recognize whether you are motivated by fear or faith. Taking action requires you to step out of the world of the known, the certain, the guaranteed, and into a world of unlimited possibility.

RECOGNIZING THE DIFFERENCE BETWEEN FEAR AND INTUITIVE RESISTANCE

Often when we are presented with new actions to take, we face a certain amount of emotion as well. When moving into a realm that is unknown to us, one of the most common emotions we face is that of fear. As a deepening aspect of our precision, learning to recognize the difference between fear and intuitive resistance is very important.

For most people, fear is a highly charged, sometimes painful sensation that is hard to ignore, and for many of us it has the power to limit or even incapacitate us. However, there is a deep benefit to this powerful expression of energy — it is there to let us know that we have had a thought or recognized a belief that has cut us off from the alignment and connection to our higher wisdom. The discomfort is there to get our attention and to notify us that in some way or another we have disconnected from our true power and are telling ourselves a distorted story that does not align with the truth of who we really are or what we are capable of.

When you feel fear, it is important to recognize it — not so that you allow it to shut you down or stop you from taking action, but rather so that you can become aware that a certain thought or belief would best be altered or diminished in some way.

When you notice yourself experiencing fear, stop and ask yourself, "What story am I telling myself that is not aligned with what my higher self knows to be true?" Remember that our highest intelligence is life affirming, constantly expanding, and ever evolving — and it knows no limitations physically or spiritually. Once you recognize the distortion you have been practicing you can gently release it and refocus your attention on the foundation and energy of peace and well-being. Then, from this stable platform, you can feel open and inspired once more to take action.

Intuitive resistance, on the other hand, is a very different sensation. The aversion to action I am speaking of in this case is the feeling that we've encountered an energetic "stop sign," when our intuition is guiding us to wait, step back, and allow timing or other details to fall into place, or to reevaluate the situation. Intuitive resistance, unlike fear, does not hurt and it does not constrict; it simply offers us a sensation that makes moving forward or taking action in any way feel limited. It's sort of like an invisible wall or barrier or an unseen arm holding us back. This resistance is a message from our intuitive wisdom, not a distortion from our lower mind, and so while it does feel as if we should wait or not act, we notice it as a neutral, stable, and balanced sensation. Not one that makes us feel bad in our skin.

This is intuitive wisdom working at its best and supporting us in right action and the path of least resistance. It is crucial, at this juncture, when you are preparing to act based on your intuitive guidance, that you learn the powerful difference between these two signals. One will prevent you from achieving any result, and the other will, in its own powerful way, even if it has guided you to wait, propel you toward that result.

BEING WILLING TO FAIL

Know this: even when an intuitive investigation alongside law enforcement, or an attempt to bring home a missing child, is successful, there will still be a certain amount of information that came through the intuitive work that was *not* accurate or that did not lead to a tangible result. Even the best intuitive practitioners in the world are not 100 percent spot-on all the time.

One of the greatest misconceptions about using intuition to achieve greater success or create a certain outcome is that it's a one-shot process that guarantees success every time. It is a bunch of little moves, sourced in the dynamic of a desired result, that work together as a complete unit over time. Some intuitive work yields immediate and tangible results; some doesn't. Your job is to continue to focus on your goal and ultimate outcome, maintain your peace, and move ahead.

If you find that a certain action is not gaining any results, then let it go. Do not try to force it, manipulate it, or make it into something it is not. Remember that intuitive information aligns itself with the energetic principle of "the path of least resistance," so if you find yourself trying to force the outcome of a particular action, you can be pretty certain that it is not in your best interests at this time. Do not take this to mean that you will never get another shot at it, however, because life is eternally generous and constantly successful. There will be unlimited opportunities to meet your goal or succeed in your efforts, but they may not appear in the same way that they did the first time you were offered the direction.

Your success in perceiving guidance and taking appropriate action will improve over time, which is not a testament to your brilliance or psychic giftedness but is instead a beneficial symptom of your dedication to developing your creative vision through practice. To choose *not* to act will stand as a greater obstacle to the possibility of who you can become, more than any disaster driven by heartfelt action ever will.

NAVIGATING THE "IN-BETWEEN"

As you start to make inner changes in thought, emotion, and awareness, and as you begin to consistently follow the directions of your intuitive mind, a time will come when it will feel as if you are smack-dab in the middle of nowhere. This is the place where visionaries often find themselves: at the point where they can no longer see the shoreline of what used to be, but not yet far enough along in the journey so that they can see the shoreline of the new world.

This place can be the most frightening part of creating any new destiny. For many people, this is the point where fear kicks in and the lower mind does whatever it can to convince them that the decision to follow this path of intuition, and to trust their unseen source of wisdom, was the most foolish thing ever. Many people will panic and revert back to their old lives, habits, and ways of being, just so they can have something solid to grasp on to.

The middle of such a change — when a system becomes highly unstable and a shift occurs that suddenly organizes that system into a higher complexity — is where evolution occurs. This is the symbolic place of dissolution and chaos, where the lowly caterpillar passes a point of no return, becomes the chrysalis, and dissolves, losing all semblance of what it used to be. Hidden in the dark cocoon of change, however, a powerful metamorphosis is occurring, obscured from view yet perfectly timed in response to an inherent and evolutionary need to become a butterfly.

If we remember that all things in life exist around us at all times, and that it is only a matter of whether our mind is ready to perceive them, then our faith in the process will allow us to maintain the state of mind necessary to bring our desire to fruition. In the past we trusted material things to move us forward; however, in this place of being neither here nor there, we must trust in the things not yet perceived by our physical senses. At this point in our journey, our most important action is to continue to rely on the foundation of peace, perception, and precision we built and to continue to choose, choose, and choose again to focus on the destiny we desire. In the midst of uncertainty, the wisest decision we can make is to look again at the mountaintop and declare once more, "I am going there."

As always, the choice is up to you.

EXERCISE
PLAY IT FORWARD

This is an easy, intuitive exercise to use when you must make a choice about a specific direction, or when you want to decide if one option is more appropriate than another. You can, in fact, use this exercise for anything that requires a decision, especially if you like the idea of having more than one possibility but you know that you have space in your life for only one.

Let's say you must choose whether to take a particular job offer. You know all the details involved, but still you are not certain if it is appropriate for you. Take a moment to get quiet, settled, and coherent; generate your foundation of peace. Become fully aware of your own inner field of energy. Let go of any preconceived notions you may have about taking the job — good, bad, or indifferent. Set your intention. Use your conscious mind to direct where your intuition will take you.

This statement about choice might help: "It is my intention to use the power of my intuitive intelligence to show me whether this job aligns with my highest good at this time." If you want to simplify it, you can shorten it to: "Please show me if this job is aligned with my highest good at this time." Create an "ask" that feels comfortable and easy for you based on the parameters of precision.

Now imagine yourself already in the job, and in your mind play it forward three months. Say to yourself, "I see myself at this new job three months from now." Even if you cannot "see" it in your inner vision, create the feeling of being there in your mind, heart, and body. Notice what you notice. Now say to yourself, "I see myself at this new job six months from now." Notice what you notice. Then say to yourself, "I see myself at this new job twelve months from now." Notice what you notice.

If the impressions you get align with what you have already determined are your signals for "yes" or "go," then it is safe to say that it is a beneficial choice for you to take the position. On the other hand, if you notice the feelings that you have identified as "no," "stop," or "wait," then you may be better served by gathering more information or passing on the opportunity.

You can also use this exercise when you have more than

one option in any particular situation — for example, when you have been offered two jobs and need to decide on one, or you really like two apartments or houses and you can choose only one. Play out the three-month, six-month, and twelve-month scenarios for the first choice. Notice what you notice. Then take a moment to clear your mind by taking a few deep breaths. Settle back into your coherence and play out the three-month, six-month, and twelve-month scenarios for the second choice. Then compare how the scenarios feel to you.

If both scenarios feel "off" to you, then you should consider that perhaps neither one is in your best interests at this time, and that there is something else around the corner that will be the precise fit. If one feels more aligned with your "yes," then consider making that your choice.

If both scenarios feel equally good to you, then simply say to yourself, "I know that either of these two opportunities will serve my best interests, and I know that whichever one I choose, I will thrive. I release this thought to the power of my intuitive mind and know that it is guiding me to the wisest choice." Then release that thought and go about your day. Know that when the moment comes to make the appropriate decision, whatever choice you make will be the correct one.

Reality versus Reality TV

I used this exercise when I had two potentially great opportunities to consider, both of which promised to have a major influence on the level of success I would have in my career. On the one hand, I had the opportunity to develop and be featured in a reality TV series that would highlight the work of intuitive detectives. On the other hand, I had the opportunity to take all my research on intuition, and the work I had done while training the police, and write this book and have it published.

Each option offered a great opportunity. Both options would allow me to pursue my passion for intuitive study and practice. And both had the potential to put me in front of a wider audience and convey my message of intuitive intelligence. On the outside they seemed like equal opportunities, but I had time to do only one. So I used the "play it forward" exercise and, well, you know which one I chose, because you are holding the result in your hands.

When I played the "reality TV" opportunity in my mind, it felt awful — claustrophobic and limiting. Even with the perceived outward benefits of possible fame and celebrity, it just felt wrong for me.

When I played the "book" opportunity in my mind, it felt peaceful, invigorating, and expansive. The book route may be less glamorous, but it felt right for me. It became a no-brainer; the message was clear. Without a regret or hesitation, I stepped out of the process of developing content for TV and turned to the process of putting First Intelligence out into the world.

Of course, if someone else had the same two opportunities and played them forward, their results might be completely different, and what might be appropriate for *them* would not be what is appropriate for *me*. Keep that in mind when someone tells you what to do on the basis of what did or did not work out for *them* in the past, advising you to expect it to be the same for you. Nonsense! You are your own unique energetic force field, and only your higher mind and soul should have any say about what's in your best interests.

The "play it forward" exercise will help you make decisions and take action from a grounded and peaceful place, which is, as you know by now, the source of your greatest power.

CHAPTER 16

STEP 7:
FRUITION

*With an eye made quiet by the power of harmony, and the deep power of joy,
we see into the life of things.*

— WILLIAM WORDSWORTH

Fruition is the final stage in the intuitive process. It is the part of
the journey when we start to see signs of the energetic seeds
we have planted beginning to tenderly appear. At this point in the
process our only duties are to maintain the energetic foundation we
have built on peace, precision, and perception and to allow the process to continue to unfold without interference.

We have dedicated our time and energy to this journey so we
can bring something into being that didn't exist before. If we have
stayed true to the principles explained in the process, then we will
realize that energetic desire, as surely as the sprout of a tiny plant
breaks free of its solid shell and the dark earth to be revealed in the
light. Fruition, like all the other intuitive processes we have reviewed
so far, has a physical and an energetic aspect to it. The definition
of the physical aspect of *fruition* provides the most common understanding of the word: it is the attainment of something desired. But
a second part of the definition, along with the word's source, reveals

the energetic aspect that holds a valuable key. That second part of the definition is: "The *enjoyment* of this [fruition]" — a definition that stems from the Latin root of the word, *frui*, which means "to enjoy." The key word here is *enjoy!*

We interfere with the fruition process when we shift into worry and anxiety, which are generated by the need to control the outcome. When we get up from our meditation and immediately return to our distorted patterns of fear and negative thinking, we essentially dig up all the seeds we planted during our intuitive practice.

In order for our intuition to serve us by providing answers that guide us to an ultimate outcome, we must be energetically aligned with that outcome as much as possible. We must — through conscious choice, focus, and sometimes sheer force of will — align all our energetic properties with our chosen goal.

To *achieve* fruition, we must *be* fruition. Our mind must constantly be the fertile soil that promotes the growth of what we desire; we must remain joyfully responsible for our energetic "dirt." If we stay committed to that elevated level of horticulture, we can rest assured that when the mind is ready, the result will appear.

You tend your energetic garden by pulling out the weeds that take shape as negative and destructive feelings and emotions. You also maintain the expanded understanding that the DNA within each tiny seed holds all the information needed to sprout that seed. And you must do your part with a sense of joy, ease, and calm expectation, knowing that there is a structure to this process and you have maintained it.

EMPOWERED SURRENDER

At this point in the process you surrender to the wisdom and power of your intuitive mind, and you let go of any ideas about how or when the first signs of new life are going to spring forth. We surrender to the wisdom of a seed when we plant it. We know that if we do our part to energetically support that seed, it will do its part and, when the time is right, the sprout will appear. But let's take a look at this word *surrender*.

Surrender is *not* about taking your hands off the wheel of your destiny; it is *not* about giving up control of your energetic responsibility. It is not about saying, "I will let the universe decide what is best for me." You must still use the power of choice to direct your path, and you must still use your will and focus to navigate the journey. Empowered surrender comes in when you stop needing to know *how* it will show up, *when* it will show up, and *what* it will look like when it does. This surrender is the willingness to let go of the limited ideas of the lower mind and to allow the ultimate creative power of the superconscious to do its job.

Remember that this level of onboard intelligence is so wise that it guides the energetic functions of all 100 trillion cells — it grows our nails, digests our food, heals the cut on our foot, rotates the planets, generates new species of life, and shapes new galaxies, all without our having a single conscious thought about it. And it does it with perfect creative beauty, balance, and ease.

This energetic form of surrender gives us a far greater source of power than grasping, manipulating, or attempting to control things ever could. When we try to control, we limit our experience of joy. When we try to force an outcome, we obliterate our ability to create new solutions. When we worry about how things are going to turn out, we cut off all the higher energy of the creative spirit; and the pressure of this worry leads to frustration, stagnation, and anxiety.

When we cling to things — including a vision of the way we think things should happen — and we stay stubbornly committed to a specific path, we tie ourselves in energetic knots. Then the creative energy needed to cultivate a new outcome is not free to move through us.

So what would it be like if you could surrender and allow all the energies that want to be expressed through you creatively, monetarily, or romantically to move through you in a way that perhaps you and your limited perspective do not have images for? The energy that you would free up would blow your mind wide open. And as you now know, the mind *must* be ready in order for the intuitive answers to appear.

Empowered surrender can be a battle of wills — the will of the lower, limited mind versus the stronger, more subtle will of the higher mind that created the desire in the first place. Some people call this level of will the Divine, but for many people this is too loaded a word. So in our conversation we can use the term *cosmic will*. But, just as a reminder, this higher level of will is *not* the game plan of some invisible old man in the sky who has a mysterious idea for your life. This cosmic will is the energetic source of your dreams and desires, and, as an equal partner in the process, it stands ready, willing, and able to assist you in bringing those desires into being. *Your* will is not separate from *its* will; but because it is part of a higher level of mind, it presents broader, more evolutionary, groundbreaking, and life-altering solutions to guide you to higher outcomes. *This* is the intelligence we choose to draw upon when creating our new destiny.

COSMIC WILL AND THE ACORN

Cosmic will is the energy that allows everything in creation to come to fruition. It is what causes the mighty oak to grow from the tiny seed; it guides it to germinate, sprout, push its roots and branches out, and grow into the tree that eventually becomes the forest.

When you hold an acorn in the palm of your hand, you don't immediately consider what is possible for it. But housed in the dark interior of that seed is the potential for millions of trees and millions

of forests. Every energetic imagining that this acorn has for itself —
which there is no physical evidence of at this moment in time — is
completely and totally supported within the field of all possibility
and is fully aligned with cosmic will.

The acorn does not fight when snow covers it or resist when rain
washes it from its base in the soil. It may get pummeled and plowed
under repeatedly, but sooner or later, when the timing is right and
the surrounding elements are aligned, the oak sprouts out of its small
cocoon of limitation and begins the process of becoming a forest.

You are no different from that acorn. Within your energetic
blueprint, you have all the bits and pieces, codes and diagrams, that
you need to grow to whatever heights you desire, to become whatever you wish to become, and to create whatever you wish to create.
No questions asked.

The Never-Ending Story

Realize, too, that fruition is *not* the final step. The place that an acorn
gets to when it finally achieves its goal to become an oak tree may
look like a great success but is only a *part* of the story. And the same
is true of your fruition.

When you have successfully used your intuitive intelligence
to reach your current goal, there will still be more seeds for you to
sow, more steps for you to take, more goals and dreams and aspira-
tions for you to pursue *after* that original fruition. When the acorn
has become the one-hundred-foot tree, it continues to throw down
new acorns, doesn't it? Simply reaching the goal does not end the
journey.

An empowered surrender will benefit you when you engage
with your current goal with a light touch. This becomes much easier when you realize that this goal is a source of more goals: it is a
dream that produces more dreams. When you can surrender to the

understanding that no matter what you're trying to reach right now, there will be more to follow, and more to follow, and more to follow — in this lifetime and in the lifetimes to come — a sense of appreciation for the perfection of the journey unfolds and your adventure becomes one of great ease and enjoyment along the way.

Nobody ever tells you that when your dreams reach fruition there will be — if you're doing it *right* — more dreams and more seeds to plant. You will dream more dreams, which will drop more acorns. And after those dreams come to fruition, there will be still more and more and more dreams — but not in a greedy, clingy, grasping way. It will be in an "Oh my goodness, isn't this fun?" kind of way.

Our lives are an unfolding. This process of success and life and rebirth is constant revelation. Each time an acorn sprouts a new oak tree, it drops back into the dirt to start all over again. Each time we make a choice to follow a certain desire, we do the same thing. We are reborn over and over and over again in this very same lifetime.

You can look back on your own life now and see where you were when you were eight years old, and see what you imagined for yourself. You are not the same person you were then. Our dreams and desires are constantly evolving; we are constantly evolving; and it is a privilege to do so.

I encourage you to consciously engage in this process of evolution, and I invite you to *enjoy* the process. The higher, more spiritual vibrations of joy, happiness, ease, laughter, patience, generosity, and peace are the energies that will sustain and support you as you grow. Recall what we learned at the beginning of this chapter: fruition = joy; joy = fruition.

THE MONKEYS KNOW

Spider monkeys that live in the rain forests of East Africa are powerful examples of fruition and surrender. They swing from vine to vine in search of their favorite berries, which grow in particular areas of the forest; and the journey is joyful. They may hang out in one tree for a while, pick a few fleas off a friend, and move on. Then they may stop again, take a wee nap, pick a few leaves off a branch, enjoy the juicy flavor, and once again move on, never becoming committed or attached to the place where they land at any given time.

When the monkeys are swinging from branch to branch, they have nothing really solid to hold on to. They have no prearranged plan that tells them where the next branch they need in order to move forward will be. Yet there is a complete and total flexibility empowered by the forward momentum that their vision has provided them.

Once in a while, they might miss a branch and tumble to the ground, but they don't stay there for long. They get up, they climb the tree again, and they move ahead. Others do not judge their tumble, they do not become anxious about the delay, there is no desperation in the journey, and the berries are still there, waiting.

We are so conditioned by the false idea that if we are not *doing* and *pursuing* and *pushing* — "Where's the branch I need? I need a damn branch!" — then we won't have the sustenance or the resources we will need to feed and clothe ourselves. But this is, once again, only the limited perspective of the lower mind. The intuitive power of our higher mind is an efficient, effective system that supports every life-form on the planet.

In developing the power of our First Intelligence, we reinvent the idea of what is truly efficient. Our deep understanding of the power of surrendering to the wisdom of our higher mind guides us to appreciate where our resources really come from. Our true resources are not external. Our true resources are not material. Our most powerful resources are internal, invisible, and wired deeply into our being, as in the cases of the acorn and the monkey.

And if it were possible for the acorn and the monkey to have a moment together, the outcome would still be good. Even if things seemed dire because the monkey spied the acorn and ate it, the brilliant power of cosmic will would still be at work. Eventually the monkey would poop the seed out, and the acorn, with all its potential, would land somewhere it would have never arrived at on its own.

EMBRACING NEW LIFE

When we learn how to use every aspect of our lives, not just the happy, pleasant parts, we find purpose and meaning in everything we have ever experienced. In such moments of elevated awareness and understanding, we recognize the light hidden in the shadows, and we rise above the hurt, anger, and frustration that may have once dominated our world.

Moments of revelation turn us into an observer of the circumstances in our life, and we shift our awareness to the "peace point," which I discussed earlier, as the source of our truest and deepest power. We discover our expanded potential to experience joy, appreciation, and grace regardless of where we might have come from and despite what life has given us so far. On this foundation our intuition stands.

At these precise moments fruition happens. The physical dynamics and spiritual energies combine to give birth to a new life. All the creation that was hidden from view suddenly becomes visible in our physical reality. When we recognize this, we celebrate it, we honor it, and we experience joy. And so it should be.

Congratulate yourself for what you have created, even if it is only the tiniest of outcomes. We all start small. Acknowledge the supreme power intrinsic to you — within your DNA and within the creative supertechnology of every aspect of your mind — which has brought you to this moment.

Your ability to generate a specific outcome by virtue of your choice, will, and empowered focus has elegantly carved you out of a vast, mediocre herd and propelled you into an adventure in creativity and power that is unlikely to be matched by those who do not understand or follow the process.

The moment you made the commitment to follow this intuitive path, you changed the trajectory of your life. You cannot know for sure how the remainder of it is meant to unfold, but I promise you that if you stay committed to the journey ahead, you will be rewarded with surprises, blessings, and discoveries that to your former, limited mind would have seemed impossible or even magical. To the new and improved you, with your expanded point of view, these are now normal, everyday expectations.

I invite you to promise yourself that, from this moment forward, you will pursue with power and confidence every dream or desire you have for the future, and that you will trust all the gifts at your disposal.

When you master your creative intuitive power and allow it to lead and support you in life, you will never knock on the door of creation as a beggar. Instead you will enter as a king.

CONCLUSION

MEETING YOUR DESTINY

The privilege of a lifetime is being who you are.

— JOSEPH CAMPBELL

Now you know what your intuitive intelligence equipment is. You know how it is structured, what it does, and how to use it. You know how to apply this powerful biological and spiritual technology to your current situation, and you know what you must do to implement the strategies and information it will provide in order to bring your desires into being.

Are you ready for what your life might be from now on? When I teach my workshops or do my coaching sessions, people often ask me, "What will I do when I achieve everything I set out to do?" I tell them, "Brace yourself," because it takes great courage to accept the energetic responsibility of becoming the architect of your destiny.

In order to use your intuition to create the life that you really wish to have, you may find that you must let go of certain things, relationships, and attitudes. More important still is the reality that using First Intelligence to assist you in creating success will require you to become someone greater than you have been. You will be required to become more of who you truly are.

If that were not a prerequisite, then you would already be living your desire. And if it were easy, everybody would be doing it. Fewer than 5 percent of the people who say they want to change for the better, or who say they want greater happiness, better health, or more joy, actually do what is required to achieve it. Only 5 percent! This is because change, no matter how awesome or beneficial it may be, isn't always comfortable. And human beings are notorious creatures of habit.

Yet we have the capacity to create lives of amazing beauty, awesome potential, and limitless joy. I would like you to view your changes, and even some of the discomfort you may feel as you move ahead in your intuitive practice, as part of a grand adventure — the hero's adventure, in which you finally become who you are meant to be.

Can you imagine what your new life might be like after successfully completing your hero's adventure and creating your chosen destiny? What do you hope to learn about yourself in order to make it an everyday part of who you are? What do you hope to bring to others? Are you really willing to live a new life in which things may never be the same again?

If you answer yes to any of these questions, then you are ready. It is your time. And so, if you haven't already, I invite you to answer the call. Your destiny is waiting.

THE POINT OF CHOICE

Your decision to change your life and to cultivate the power to design your future began long before you and I ever crossed paths. Chances are pretty good that your desire to discover who you are truly meant to be, and to use this discovery to improve your life and the lives of others, has been on your mind for quite a while now. I am willing to bet that you received the call to create your own destiny a long time ago.

At this stage of your journey, you are ready to receive this work and discover the tools that will link you to your true creative power. When the student is ready, the teaching or the teacher *does* appear. I am so glad to have been an ally and an assistant on your intuitive adventure.

You now have, and always have had, access to the only tools you will ever need. And, as you have learned while studying the facets of this process, when you make an empowered choice, align it with the power of your integrated mind and body, and allow the power of your intuitive wisdom to direct you, then, even if you do not arrive exactly where you expected to, you should consider yourself hugely successful just by virtue of the things you have learned and the power you have gained along the way.

Like the caterpillar that must completely alter itself in order to become a butterfly, you have made a commitment to no longer crawl through your life, but to fly instead.

I thank you for allowing me to be a small part of your adventure. I wish you ultimate joy, happiness, peace, and success as you continue to reach beyond the old boundaries of limitation to look into the deepest reservoirs of your wisdom and inner certainty. The word *courage* comes from the word *coeur*, which means "heart." I invite you to use your heart well in every moment, because it will serve you and reward you in ways you may have only dreamed of. The road to one's destiny is not random, nor is it fate. It is determined by choice — choice informed by wisdom, trust, and courage.

ACKNOWLEDGMENTS

It is said that the life of an artist or writer is a solitary one, but the process of bringing this book to life has been the result of the actions of a large number of people who have contributed in a myriad of selfless ways to bring it to fruition. I am blessed to be surrounded by a group of creative and compassionate people who time and time again have moved me with their graciousness.

I would like to express my most sincere appreciation, love, and gratitude to my friends Ali Laventhol, Heather Talty, Scott Tejerian, Amy Berkholtz, and Ducky Punch — the beloved members of my chosen family who have encouraged, supported, and inspired me. I am continually moved by your level of generosity and kindness. I would not have been able to complete this part of my journey without you, and I love you all.

I am grateful as well to my creative team at New World Library — Kristen Cashman, Bonita Hurd, Kim Corbin, Munro Magruder, Ami Parkerson, Tona Pearce Myers, and Tracy Cunningham, who each contributed in their special way to assist me in bringing my best work into the world. An added dollop of gratitude goes to my editor, Georgia Hughes, who brought grace and clarity to the process of bringing *First Intelligence* to life.

I would also like to thank my dear friends and art collectors who have been a part of my creative journey since it began almost twenty years ago and who were an integral part of providing the time and freedom I needed to dedicate almost two years to creating this book. A special note of gratitude goes to Doug Hart and Carole Laventhol, whose generosity and support throughout this process will be forever appreciated.

My deepest appreciation goes to Michael Saunders and Steve Burton. Thank you for the courage you exhibited and the faith you had in me to bring such a boundary-pushing program into the world of law enforcement. You may never really know how much your belief in me has changed my life.

I would like to thank all the men and women who have attended my workshops, read my books, and come to me for personal coaching sessions. You inspire me with your courage and dedication to life. Thank you for putting your faith in the work I do; it has brought meaning to my journey, and I am grateful.

And, last, to my beloved furry children, Lily and Harley, who have shown me the healing power of unconditional love and the transformative influence of living in the moment, and who have shared with me the sheer bliss of playing ball on a sunny day and lying in the grass to watch the flowers bloom. Thank you for being such wonderful teachers; you have both filled my life with joy and made me a better human being.

ENDNOTES

INTRODUCTION

1. Richard Alleyne, "Welcome to the Information Age," *The Telegraph* (United Kingdom), February 2011, www.telegraph.co.uk/science /science-news/8316534/Welcome-to-the-information-age-174 -newspapers-a-day.html.

CHAPTER 1. YOUR TRILATERAL INTELLIGENCE SYSTEM

1. Arnold B. Scheibel, "Embryological Development of the Human Brain," Johns Hopkins School of Education website, 1997, www.education.jhu .edu/PD/newhorizons/Neurosciences/articles/Embryological%20 Development%20of%20the%20Human%20Brain/.
2. John F. Neas, "The Tissue Level of Organization," in *Embryology Atlas* (New York: Pearson Education, 2003), chap. 3, http://cwx.prenhall.com /bookbind/pubbooks/martini10/chapter3/custom3/deluxe-content.html.
3. "Physiology of the Pineal Gland," CNS Clinic-Jordan-Neurosurgery web-site, undated, www.neuroradiology.ws/pinealomasphysiology.htm.
4. Emma Young, "Gut Instincts: The Secrets of Your Second Brain," *New*

Scientist, no. 2895 (December 17, 2012), www.newscientist.com/article/mg21628951.900-gut-instincts-the-secrets-of-your-second-brain.html.

5.   Institute of HeartMath, *Science of the Heart: Exploring the Role of the Heart in Human Performance*, Institute of HeartMath website, undated, www.heartmath.org/research/science-of-the-heart/introduction.html.

6.   Institute of HeartMath, "Heart-Brain Interactions," *Institute of HeartMath Newsletter* 10, no. 1 (Spring 2011), www.heartmath.org/templates/ihm/e-newsletter/publication/2011/spring/heartmath-definition.php.

CHAPTER 2. THE HIDDEN WISDOM OF DNA

1.   Bruce Lipton, *Beliefs, Genes, Genetic Determinism, Genetics, Perceptions*, YouTube, December 1, 2012, www.youtube.com/watch?v=lSo88GMrA8w.

2.   Cleve Backster, "Evidence of a Primary Perception in Plant Life," *International Journal of Parapsychology* 10, no. 4 (Winter 1968), www.rebprotocol.net/clevebaxter/Evidence%20of%20a%20Primary%20Perception%20In%20Plant%20Life%2023pp.pdf.

3.   Luc Montagnier et al., "DNA, Waves and Water," *Journal of Physics: Conference Series* 306, no. 1 (2011), www.arxiv.org/PS_cache/arxiv/pdf/1012/1012.5166v1.pdf.

4.   B. Göhler et al., "Spin Selectivity in Electron Transmission through Self-Assembled Monolayers of Double-Stranded DNA," *Science* 331, no. 6019 (February 18, 2011): 894–97.

5.   Mark Pilkington, "Primary Perception," *The Guardian*, June 9, 2004, www.theguardian.com/education/2004/jun/10/research.highereducation4.

6.   Rollin McCraty, Mike Atkinson, and Dana Tomasino, "Modulation of DNA Conformation by Heart-Focused Intention," Institute of Heart Math, 2003, www.heartmath.org/templates/ihm/downloads/pdf/research/publications/modulation-of-dna.pdf.

CHAPTER 3. THE POWER OF THE UNIFIED FIELD

1.   John S. Hagelin, *Is Consciousness the Unified Field? A Field Theorist's Perspective* (Fairfield, IA: Maharishi University of Management, undated), www.mum.edu/pdf_msvs/v01/hagelin.pdf.

2.   "The Gold Foil Experiment: Ernest Rutherford," http://chemed.chem.purdue.edu/genchem/history/gold.html; www.physics.rutgers.edu/meis/Rutherford.htm.

CHAPTER 4. PEACE

1. Edgar Mitchell, "Quantum Theory, the Quantum Hologram and Zero Point Energy," Quantrek, undated, www.quantrek.com/Zero_point _energy/Zero_point_energy.htm.
2. "Coherence," Institute of HeartMath, 2012, www.heartmath.org/research /research-home/coherence.html.
3. Rollin McCraty, Mike Atkinson, and Dana Tomasino, *Science of the Heart: Exploring the Role of the Heart in Human Performance,* publication no. 10-001 (Boulder Creek, CA: Institute of HeartMath, 2001), www.heartmath.org /research/science-of-the-heart/introduction.html.

CHAPTER 11. STEP 2: ACCESSING THE FIELD

1. "About the Global Coherence Initiative," Global Coherence Initiative, undated, www.glcoherence.org/about-us/about.html.
2. Charles Sabine, "Senses Helped Animals Survive the Tsunami," *NBC News,* January 6, 2005, www.today.com/id/6795562/ns/today/t/senses-helped -animals-survive-tsunami/#.Ui7oJb-AQ3U.
3. "About the Global Coherence Monitoring System," Global Coherence Initiative, undated, www.glcoherence.org/monitoring-system/about -system.html.

CHAPTER 14. STEP 5: INTERPRETATION

1. Sharon L. Lechter and Greg S. Reid, *Three Feet from Gold* (New York: Sterling, 2009).

INDEX

mind as biological antenna in,
    98–99, 98 *fig. 10*
in mythology, 41
operation of, 37–39, 38 *fig. 2*
scientific theory behind, 35–36
supernormal mental phenomena
    explained through, 36–37
understanding, 43–44
unity consciousness, 124
universal grid, 36
Universal Mind, 36
universal wisdom, connection to,
    124–29, 126 *fig. 16*
universe
    as alive, 37
    mental (conscious) nature of,
        35–37
University of Southern California, 3

vacuum, 39
vagus nerve, 19

vibration, 148–49
visionaries, 7
visionary certainty, 121
visionary power, 121–24, 122 *fig. 15*

wave functions, 37–38, 38 *fig. 2*
"why" questions, 166
"will I?" questions, 167
wishful thinking, 68
women's intuition, 192
Wordsworth, William, 226
worry, 64
writing, 195–97

Yeats, William Butler, 183

zero point, 57, 60
"zone, the," 65

ABOUT THE AUTHOR

As a preeminent authority on intuitive intelligence and creativity, Simone Wright is an internationally recognized expert on the power of the human mind and its massive potential for evolutionary intelligence and groundbreaking ingenuity. She is a highly respected intuitive consultant, lifelong entrepreneur, and award-winning artist who has become the bestselling artist of her kind in the world.

Simone's client list includes the top achievers and emerging talents in a broad field of specialties in private and public enterprises. From law enforcement personnel to elite athletes, from health care providers to Hollywood entertainers, and from corporate CEOs to groundbreaking entrepreneurs, all have benefited from Simone's precise intuitive vision.

Simone has written articles for several magazines, appeared on radio and television programs across North America, presented keynote speeches at numerous conferences, and been featured on *The Oprah Winfrey Show.*

When not busy writing or teaching, Simone continues to create award-winning artwork in her studio in Los Angeles. See her artwork at www.simonewrightfineart.com.

Information about her workshops and coaching can be found at www.simonewright.com.